Builders
& Fools

Derek J. Tidball

Builders & Fools

Leadership the Bible way

inter-varsity press

INTER-VARSITY PRESS
38 De Montfort Street, Leicester LE1 7GP, England

First published 1999
Reprinted 1999

British Library Cataloguing in Publication Data
A catalogue record for this book is available from the British Library.

ISBN 0–85111–592–6

Typeset in Great Britain
Printed and bound in Great Britain by Creative Design and Print (Wales), Ebbw Vale.

Inter-Varsity Press is the book-publishing division of the Universities and Colleges Christian Fellowship (formerly the Inter-Varsity Fellowship), a student movement linking Christian Unions in universities and colleges throughout Great Britain, and a movement of the International Fellowship of Evangelical Students. For information about local and national activities write to UCCF, 38 De Montfort Street, Leicester LE1 7GP.

Contents

A Prayer

Lord, you have placed me in your church as overseer and pastor. You see how unfit I am to administer this great and difficult office. Had I previously been without help from you, I would have ruined everything long ago. Therefore I call upon you. I gladly offer my mouth and heart to your service. I would teach the people and I would continue to learn. To this end I shall meditate diligently on your Word. Use me, dear Lord, as your instrument. Only do not forsake me; for if I were to continue alone, I would quickly ruin everything. Amen.

Luther's *Lectures on Genesis*, chs. 26 – 30 (1542), quoted by Thomas Oden, *Becoming a Minister*, Classical Pastoral Care (New York: Crossroads, 1987), p. 47.

Introduction

The pastor[1] has resigned. What is the church to do? It has become fashionable when this happens for churches to appoint a search committee, whose first task is to draw up a job description. The document, which is then circulated to bishops, moderators or superintendents, and prospective candidates alike, usually contains a description of the church, together with its needs as the committee sees them; a list of the tasks a new pastor is expected to undertake, possibly listed in some form of priority; the qualities a candidate will need to possess, and some comments about terms and conditions of employment or length of contract.

This 'job-description' approach to ministry is well-intentioned and has some merits. In recent years so many pastors have run into difficulties that search committees rightly want to guard themselves against disaster happening in their church, or, worse still, happening *again* in their church. Numerous factors contribute to a high casualty rate in ministry. The broken relationships which occur between pastor and people when they are working to different agendas and suffering from conflicting expectations are among them. The problem lying submerged, like a nuclear warhead carried by a silent submarine waiting to launch devastation, is that the issue of agendas and expectations has never been addressed openly. So now, it is thought, stipulating demands in a job description will prevent tragedies, and result in greater harmony and efficiency.

The road of the job description is one which is being travelled frequently today in secular business and the professions. It is not surprising therefore that it is being adopted as a practice in the church. But, as with all practices adopted from the world, spiritual discernment is needed. It does not seem to occur to many church leaders that it may not *always* be for the good of the church that good business practice be transferred over. The fundamental problem with it, I believe, is this: the work of the pastor is a calling, not a career. It arises out of a covenant relationship and not a contractual one. The road of the job description, unfortunately, encourages a career mentality and a contractual perspective in pastor and people alike.

Please do not misread me. My hesitation is not intended to put the work of the pastor (a term I shall usually use and which readers can translate into minister, vicar, bishop, elder, church leader or any other equivalent term with which they are more familiar) in a special category above that of 'ordinary' workers in secular jobs. Far from it. Pastor and people should communicate with each other and be agreed as to their expectations. Churches should spell out realistically and considerately (and generously!) the reward the pastor should receive for his or her work. The pastor should be accountable to the church for the way his or her time is spent and gifts are used. Churches, in the past, have not always been noted for the clarity of their thinking, and moves towards a sharper focus in understanding ministry is wise. And, in any case, contemporary law makes it impossible to avoid thinking in contractual terms completely, even if one would wish to do so.

Even so, the job-description approach to ministry contains a number of inherent flaws. First, the more one spells out, the more one has to spell out. It leads one down the road of contracts, sub-clauses, definitions, legalism and eventually of employment tribunals[2] and the sad spectacle of Christians suing one another. It encourages a career mentality and, with it, the counting of hours and perks, the quest for reward in proportion to responsibility and the assumption that there is a ladder to be climbed. Of course, it doesn't have to be like that. But already experience suggests it probably is.

Secondly, and more significantly, the approach fails to understand that pastoral ministry (and, indeed, any other kind of leadership in the church) is essentially about relationships, not about contract.[3] When Elizabeth Taylor divorced her eighth husband, the press immediately wanted to know what the prenuptial agreement had stipulated about the divorce settlement. How much of Elizabeth Taylor's wealth would her latest ex walk away with? Most Christians would readily see that a marriage entered into on the basis of a contract, stipulating the responsibilities of each partner, the financial arrangements and other minutiae, and which anticipated what would happen in the event of a breakup, was somewhat lacking. The element of love, of self-giving to one's partner, of growing devotion and commitment, of promise to be together 'for better, for worse, for richer, for poorer', of trust and of adventure, is missing. Marriage is a covenant, not a contract; a relationship, not a business. The same is true of the partnership between pastor and church.

The failure to understand this has been the reason, I believe, for the inability of a number of younger ministers to sustain ministry after a few years. Dissatisfaction with ministry often develops early.[4] But this is not surprising if it is entered with wrong expectations. If either the fledgling pastor or the calling church pretends it can be approached like any other job, then it is not surprising if disappointment quickly follows. We do no service to anyone by pretending the pastoral ministry can ever be like a nine-to-five job. By its nature it is different. The biblical images of pastoral ministry make this point powerfully.

The mention of 'adventure' just now gives us the clue, thirdly, to another serious fault with the job-description approach to ministry. It is sterile and lacks imagination. To be told how many sermons one must preach, how many visits one must make, how many communions one must conduct, how many meetings one must chair, how many house-groups one must teach, and so on, leaves little room for creativity, spontaneity and inspiration.

Perhaps there is another way of looking at ministry. It is here we come to the burden of this book. The New Testament is full of marvellous pictures or metaphors of pastoral ministry.[5] It is, I believe, by returning to consider some of these images that we shall regain a sense of direction in ministry and overcome something of the malaise from which many a busy pastor, labouring under the tyranny of an activist approach to ministry, suffers.

Images of pastoral ministry in recent writing

An earlier book of Alastair Campbell's, *Rediscovering Pastoral Care*,[6] introduced me to the power of images and skilfully wove some biblical and contemporary images of ministry together.

Three recent books have sought to set out contemporary images of the pastor, and these have been illuminating and fruitful. Donald Messer, in *Contemporary Images of Christian Ministry*,[7] speaks of pastors as wounded healers in the community of the compassionate, servant leaders in a servant church, political mystics in a prophetic community, enslaved liberators of the rainbow church and practical theologians in a post-denominational church.

Ian Bunting has written an insightful, if brief, survey of the issue in *Models of Ministry: Managing the Church Today*.[8] Bunting's approach relates to models of ministry rather than to images, but the boundary between the two is blurred at times. He traces the way in which the church has constantly revised its models of ministry to reflect the age in which it lives. In recent times, he comments, 'the models have followed each other with increasing rapidity'. He lists seven contemporary models: the consultant, the overseer, the competent professional, the practical theologian, the minister in community, the community builder and the middle manager. Elsewhere he speaks of the model of the therapist as having particular contemporary appeal. His personal preference, reflecting contemporary culture, is to see the minister as a pathfinder. In using the term, he seeks to rehabilitate the model of the minister as a good manager which, he recognizes, has not always been a model congenial to the clergy. Nevertheless he argues that the managerial model has great currency. He sees the three responsibilities of the pathfinder as 'establishing the identity of the church by telling the Christian story and interpreting it for the community of faith'; 'leading the people in worship' and 'using theological imagination'.[9]

More prosaically, Paul Beasley-Murray, in *A Call to Excellence*,[10] has spoken of the need for ministers to be professional pastors, effective leaders, charismatic preachers, creative liturgists, missionary strategists, senior care-givers and exemplary pilgrims.

The value of biblical images

Contemporary images are helpful. I believe, however, that we shall find a more secure set of images by returning to our biblical roots. Contemporary images, unconnected to those found in inspired Scripture, may prove illuminating but may equally be nothing but illusions. I lament, with Thomas Oden in his writing on pastoral care, the way in which we have neglected our classical roots. Early understanding of the pastoral role and rich classical resources have been set aside and replaced wholesale by whatever is modern or, even worse, merely currently in fashion. 'Evidence is growing', he writes, 'that the time is ripe for a major restudy of classical Christian pastoral care. The average pastor has come to a saturation point with fads.'[11] Amen to that. But in seeking to return to our roots, we must avoid the temptation to be reactionary. The point of the exercise is not to take us backward but to take us forward, to enrich the present by an understanding of the past and to enable us to be more fitted to meet contemporary challenges to the high calling of pastoral ministry.

Ian Bunting wisely warns that there are problems in using biblical models as a way of understanding ministerial leadership. He highlights three: first, they reflect the dominant-leader images of their age; second, it is easy to read into them what we think they mean; and third, what we say and think about ministry and what we do are two different things.[12] His cautions are wise. These models need handling with care, especially as we seek to transfer them from an ancient culture to our own. Even so, in the current climate, I would rather stress something else he says. The New Testament models, he writes, 'continue to be authoritative and formative for Christians'. I am among those to whom he refers when he says that 'many believe a return to them is the first priority of the church today'.[13]

To one of Bunting's strictures I must plead partly guilty. It is very easy to read into the images what we think they mean. But that, surely, is the advantage of an image. While it needs to be sited in its original setting and disciplined by the way its original readers would have understood it as well as by the wider sweep of Scripture – and that is what we have sought to do with every image – having done that, it is surely possible to meditate on the image from a present-day standpoint and derive legitimate understanding about modern ministry from it.

In the light of such comments, we need to understand something of the nature of 'images' and 'imagination'. In a postmodern world image is all. Advertisers seek to convey images; so much so that we are often left wondering what the product is that they are seeking to sell and that we are supposed to feel so great about. Image and substance often have little to do with each other. It is not in this way that the words 'image' and 'imagination' are being used here. Our use is more disciplined. Image is being used in the sense of metaphor. A metaphor is a way of describing one thing by reference to something else. They are not identical, but the connection between them is evident to all.

Sallie McFague has argued that the use of the metaphor 'is indigenous to Christianity, not just in the sense that it is permitted, but is called for'.[14] She points to the parables and to the gospel being expressed in the language of the kingdom of God as evidence. 'Poets', she writes, 'use metaphor all the time because they are constantly speaking about the great unknowns – mortality, love, fear, joy, guilt, hope, and so on. Religious language is deeply metaphorical for the same reason and it is therefore no surprise that Jesus' most characteristic form of teaching, the parables, should be extended metaphors.'[15]

A little later she explores the relationship between concepts and metaphors. Concepts are couched in flatter language, which tends toward 'clear and concise meanings'. Images lack the same precision and are more ambiguous and multi-levelled. Both are necessary, and one without the other is dangerous. 'Images "feed" concepts; concepts "discipline" images. Images without concepts are blind; concepts without images are sterile.'[16] In terms of ministry, much professional talk is sterile, based on concept alone without any place for spiritual imagination. But the biblical images are fertile and can lead to a new engagement with the task.

The images chosen in this book

Images, like imagination, can run away with us. So they must not be used in isolation from conceptual truth, nor, in the area we are to explore, should one image be used to the exclusion of the others. They balance one another. Isolated, any image might lead to a whole host of evils, ranging from abuse of power and authoritarianism on the one hand, to a sense of overwhelming inadequacy, overload and consequently breakdown on the other. Richness and maturity are to be found in holding the diverse images together in creative tension.

The images differ widely. Some are but a single word. Others are spoken of in depth and explored from several angles in different parts of Scripture. Some shed light on a single aspect of ministry. Others are rounded and comprehensive in their scope. The relevance and application of some are obvious. Our first impression of others is that their relevance and application might be more strained. Whatever the case, we shall approach each one from the angle that Eugene Peterson has called 'contemplative exegesis'.[17] That is, locating them first in their original setting and understanding what they would have originally meant, we shall then meditate prayerfully on them and draw out their relevance and application to our own ministries.[18] In doing so, I believe that, held together, the images will enrich our understanding and renew the vision of pastoral leadership.

The images chosen are suggestive rather than exhaustive. Some obvious ones are included to provide a balanced gallery of portraits. Other obvious ones are omitted, often because they overlap with ones which are included. Thus we include the image of builder but not that of farmer; we include that of athlete but not that of soldier. Some less obvious ones are included because they offer a penetrating challenge to contemporary thinking and practice of ministry. The image of the ambassador concentrates on the pastor's role as a messenger; that of the athlete on the need for discipline, training and determination; that of the builder makes us look at what we are building on and with; that of the fool leads us to reflect on the role we play; that of the parent highlights the dynamics of our relationships; that of the pilot brings into focus the general task of directing the church; that of scum uncomfortably sets out our status; while the image of shepherd ties them all together.

It would have been good to have included others. W. E. Chadwick's opening words in his book on *The Pastoral Teaching of St Paul*[19] were these:

> The Christian minister is a workman, not a machine; he works with certain instruments, upon a particular kind of material; and he works in order to form or fashion a certain definite object – an object with a particular definite character. But the Christian minister should be not only a workman, he must be an artist, in the highest sense of the word, by which I mean that he must be a highly skilled workman and that his personality or character must enter into his work and be impressed upon all his material.[20]

It would have been good to explore that suggestive image of the pastor as a workman, an artist, a craftsman, but a line had to be drawn.

The images are, of course, ones that Paul applies first and foremost to himself. But in a derived sense I believe they are inherited by all who follow in his footsteps in leading the church. Nothing said about them gives any indication that they are either unique to him or locked into the first century. There is a clear sense in which Paul writes of himself as a model and pattern for others.

Versions of four or five of the chapters have been presented at a number of Area Baptist Ministers' Conferences in the last few years. I am grateful for the comments and suggestions received from my colleagues in ministry on those occasions. But, of course, I alone can accept responsibility for what is now presented, with all its limitations and faults.

Questions for reflection have been added at the conclusion of each chapter in an attempt to prevent busy ministers from rushing through but not applying to themselves what they have read. They could be worked through in a group, but are designed for use primarily by individuals, hence they are written in the first person.

My last pastoral ministry was in the city of Plymouth. It is a city capable of breathtaking beauty. But for all its beauty, one has to admit that it is predominantly characterized by grey stone walling and plenty of rain – or so it seems – from October to May. Sometimes, in the busyness of a pastoral life, the grey stone walls seemed to close in and energy for ministry began to flag. On those occasions my wife and I would occasionally get in our car and drive a few miles north, out of the city, to Dartmoor. There was one spot which was always a feast for sore eyes. It was the spot where the city was left behind and where suddenly a wide vista of the moor opened up in front of us. We could see nothing but green, coarse grass – in truth, a multitude of green hues, purple heathers and grazing sheep. We could see for miles. We felt we could begin to breathe again. It restored our vision, and often our souls as well.

I pray that the images we discuss, rooted as they are in divine revelation, will restore our vision, correct our direction and deepen our understanding of pastoral ministry. My hope is for a reinvigoration of the biblical vision of ministry, rooted as it is in relationships, not contract and job description. For the benefit of pastor and people alike, I pray for a rediscovery of a sense of pastoral vocation, to the greater glory of God.

1
Ambassador

'We are ... Christ's
ambassadors ...' (2 Cor. 5:20).

The world of the ambassador seems to carry with it a faint whiff of
unreality. The idea lurches in my mind between archaic ceremonies,
as credentials are presented by formally dressed ladies and
gentlemen to the Court of St James so that they may become Ambassadors Plenipotentiary for their home countries, and the daring,
but secretive, exploits of James Bond-like figures who never get
ruffled in the most fiendish of circumstances and who always somehow come out on top. I am sure the truth is more ordinary and lies
somewhere between the two. The office is both less comic and more
significant, less exciting and more routine at one and the same time.

When Paul spoke of being an ambassador for Christ, he was
thinking in a much more straightforward way. In the political and
legal world of his day an ambassador was not usually a professional
diplomat but someone who was prepared to travel to represent a
government or community. He would carry a message and express
the views of those who had sent him. He would embody the
interests of the sending power and negotiate on its behalf.
Ambassadors were charged with finding the strategic moment and
the most effective means of communicating the message. They were

men sent to live in foreign territories. The word was used both for official imperial delegates and for those who acted as agents on behalf of small communities or even private individuals. The heart of the role was that of representation and of supplication. Prior to the days of information technology and instant communication, the ambassador was more than a mere messenger, and would often have full power to determine the position his sender would adopt. He was called upon to act in a way that he knew would meet the approval of those who had dispatched him.[1]

Twice,[2] in Paul's letters, the apostle speaks of himself as an ambassador. He is an ambassador, first, 'for Christ' (2 Cor. 5:20) and, secondly, 'of the gospel' (Eph. 6:19–20). In many ways the ambassadorial metaphor is a primary one for the apostle Paul. Since his conversion on the Damascus road and his subsequent commissioning (Acts 9:1–19), he had devoted his life to travelling where the gospel was not known and appealing to people to be reconciled to God. So these two brief phrases hide a wealth of meaning and, equally, elements of surprise as to the nature of apostolic ambassadorship.

As often, Paul takes up a metaphor from his own world and adapts it to his own ends. Anthony Bash argues that Paul's emphasis on travelling and appeal was typical of the work of the ancient ambassador.[3] But, he argues, there is little evidence that ancient ambassadors played a major role in settling disputes and bringing about reconciliation. More normally they came as representatives of weaker parties seeking to supplicate for peace. Furthermore, people in the ancient world liked to be proud of their ambassadors. The way in which Paul sets out his role as an ambassador, as we shall see, is not one which gives the Corinthians grounds for pride in him. Far from it. Rather, he sets out his role in such a way that they would almost certainly express their disapproval of him, and they did. It is for this reason that Bash concludes that though the metaphor is so appropriate for Paul's role, he does not make so much of it in his later writings.

Contemporary pastors, and indeed other Christian leaders, have inherited Paul's ambassadorial mantle, not as apostles but as leaders within the church. What, then, can we learn about being an ambassador for Christ and of the gospel?

Paul's view of the work of the ambassador is best understood by unpacking the context of 2 Corinthians 5. The relationship between the church at Corinth and Paul was anything but smooth. According to Paul, the Corinthians were not living out the gospel they claimed to believe in, since they were not at peace, either with Paul or with each other. Since he was an ambassador for Christ, it was his duty to plead with them to grasp the gospel of reconciliation. Throughout the passage, the focus of Paul's concern is on the message the ambassador has to convey. But a number of other aspects are touched upon in addition, which relate to the commission, the dignity, the motivation and the scope of the ambassador.

The commission of the ambassador

An ambassador was a person of authority because he was sent by one with greater authority. He had received a commission, and it was that commission which gave him his identity. True, he might be appropriately qualified or gifted. Ambassadors were usually people of experience and status, not least because they would have been both free and able to travel, which they often had to do at their own expense. The very word for 'ambassador',[4] coming as it does from the same family as the word for 'elder', emphasizes the prestige and maturity which would be sought in appointing someone to the role. He would need to be a seasoned person who could be trusted. He was to be a diplomat. What he said would commit the powers back home to certain stances or courses of action and the costs associated with them. Authority, then, always needed to be blended with diplomacy. But, even so, it was the commission which was all important.

In claiming the title of 'ambassador for Christ', Paul is claiming to speak the message of the gospel by commission of Christ. We see in him the tension between authority and diplomacy. In spite of the fact that he represents Christ, he does not vaunt his authority. Often, he seems to soft-peddle it by setting aside the language of command and using in its place the language of appeal.[5] He implores them 'on Christ's behalf: Be reconciled to God' (2 Cor. 5:20). He probably knows that the vocabulary of command, even if legitimate, does not always achieve its objective. Any parent with a recalcitrant child can testify to that. But when a full-frontal attack fails to gets its obstacle to yield, the gentler approach will sometimes prove more effective. So, here, in the delicate relationship between Paul and the Corinthians, although he has a right to exert apostolic authority as their founder (1 Cor. 4:15–16), he uses the more tender language of persuasion. An ambassador does not always have to wear his authority on his sleeve, nor does he always gain a hearing by undue assertiveness. The gentler approach in no way diminishes the real authority which the ambassador carries, and should not be mistaken for weakness. Rather, it illustrates that the ambassador has to be a diplomat who finds the right way and the right moment to express his message if he is to serve the one who sent him.

In spite of that, Paul makes a remarkable claim about his authority. It is daring enough to say, as Paul does, that he is speaking on behalf of God. But he goes further. Paul asserts that when he speaks, God makes his appeal through him. God is the active agent and effective speaker, while Paul is just the vocal instrument. It is God's 'voice that men and women hear and his authority that is brought to bear on people's lives'.[6] His appeal to them, whether it be through preaching, teaching or the writing of letters, is not a matter of his personal opinion or mature pastoral reflection or of trying to read God's thoughts for him and saying what he thinks God would say in the circumstances. It is the very voice of God himself. He claimed exactly the same in writing to the Thessalonians. He thanked God for them 'because, when you received the word of God, which you heard from us, you accepted it not as a human word, but as it actually is, the word of God' (1 Thess. 2:13).

The metaphor of the ambassador, then, leads us to adopt a high view of preaching. We often think that, at our best, we can be a faithful spokesperson for God. We hope we've understood and interpreted the message aright. Or, more timidly, we give a Christian reflection on X, a homily about Y, and so on. But do we any longer have a vision for preaching as an event in which God himself will communicate through us? Do we any longer have the audacity to believe that as we speak, God himself is called into play and addresses the people we address? Sidney Greidanus helps us understand how it might be so. Drawing attention to Romans 1:16 and 1 Corinthians 1:18, he writes:

Contemporary preaching of the gospel … is an indispensable link in the chain of God's redemptive activity which runs from Old Testament times to the last day (Matt. 24:14). God uses contemporary preaching to bring his salvation to people today, to build his church, to bring in his kingdom. In short, contemporary biblical preaching is nothing less than a redemptive event.[7]

Then he adds wisely, 'this high view of preaching can never be the boast of preachers, of course; it can only underscore their responsibility'. The preacher, then, like the ambassador, has authority to convey a message on behalf of a sovereign. Unlike the ambassador, his or her words are not mere words. They are living, active and effective, and through them, assuming the preacher's message is consistent with the truth of God, God himself speaks and works. To be an ambassador for Christ is to partake in a much more dynamic mode of communication than any traditional ambassador will ever do. The ordinary ambassador's words are significant. They carry the weight of the sovereign represented, and the sovereign's action will back them up. But more is being claimed here about the true ambassador of Christ. God, himself, works in the passing on of the message to bring about transformation, redemption and salvation. These words are living and effective. And that is an awesome responsibility for any human being to assume.

The dignity of the ambassador

Dignity often goes hand in hand with authority. The word for 'ambassador', as we have mentioned, comes from the same family of words as that for 'elder'. For obvious reasons ambassadors would not usually have been chosen from among the young and inexperienced. The men chosen were usually those who had the benefit of a wealth of money and experience, the wisdom of old age and the gravitas of bearing to go with them.[8] Dignity was expected.

Dignity, as judged by our world, is certainly a characteristic in the normal diplomatic world: a world characterized by grand residences, luxurious limousines, well-trained servants, expensive clothes, impressive functions, visits to royal palaces and business in powerful offices. As a representative of a foreign power, the ambassador strives to project the right image – the image of wealth and regal security.

As Christ's ambassador, Paul is the envoy of the one who is 'the blessed and only Ruler, the King of kings and Lord of lords' (1 Tim. 6:15). Some (those who believe in a 'prosperity gospel', for example) take this to mean that he could have legitimately taken to himself the trappings of wealth and dignity. It would have been a means of sending a signal about the status of the one he represents, would it not? But Paul will have none of it. He handles the question of dignity by resorting to irony.

Paul's boast is that he is an 'ambassador in chains' (Eph. 6:20). That, as Markus Barth points out,[9] is an oxymoron, an apparently contradictory expression. Ambassadors might be in peril (not least because of the dangers of travelling), snubbed, marginalized and ignored. They might even be summoned in anger to receive the ire of a host government. But they would not be imprisoned.[10] Such a fate would be inconceivable and tantamount to an act of aggression towards the ambassador's master. But Paul asserts that this was his lot as an ambassador for Christ.

In talking of his chains, Paul pokes fun at the world of the political ambassador. They, too, wore chains. They wore chains of gold and silver to festive occasions, as signals of the impressiveness of their governments. Paul's chains were of an altogether different kind.

Yet his chains were appropriate to his office and to the King he represented. His sovereign was despised and rejected by men and women. His sovereign's crown was a crown of thorns. His royal throne was a cross of crucifixion. If Paul was truly to represent King Jesus, then prison chains, not gold chains, were a fitting sign of the dignity of his office. Those of us who rejoice in our calling as ambassadors of Jesus Christ should take note. The credentials of our office are the opposite of those expected in the normal world of diplomacy.

There is a further sense in which the ambassador is expected to exhibit dignity. As a representative of another country he is not expected to let that country down by his behaviour. Rather, he must be a worthy representative of that country and exalt its reputation in the eyes of others. When a 'league of shame' was published recently by the British Government, listing those diplomats who had committed offences in Britain but who could not be prosecuted for it because they were covered by diplomatic immunity, covering everything from drink-driving to assault and breech of the peace, a number of embassies rushed to defend themselves. One spokesperson claimed to have been very upset that the matter had been made public, since 'the commission takes a strong line with anyone who brings the name of the country into disrepute. These matters have been dealt with.'[11] Their country's reputation depends on them.

So it is with ambassadors of Christ. While Paul's perspective on the image of the ambassador highlights the message the ambassador brings, it cannot be separated from the messenger himself. Marshall McLuhan spoke truth, even if he overstated it: 'The medium is the message.' The message can so easily be overshadowed by the messenger. The two must be in harmony. The ambassador must live authentically for Christ, just as all Christians must 'live a life worthy of the calling [they] have received' (Eph. 4:1). We can never get away with being mere 'professionals' who act up to the part when necessary but deny the message by the way we live the rest of the time.

The motivation of the ambassador

Joseph Kennedy, the father of JFK, let it be known to Jimmy Roosevelt that he had an ambition to be ambassador to the United Kingdom. When Roosevelt tried to dissuade him, Kennedy persisted, saying, 'I've been thinking about it and I'm intrigued by the thought of being the first Irishman to be Ambassador from the United States to the Court of St James.'[12] After a little hesitation, it seemed that the job was his for the asking. He relished life among the upper classes of British society and was mesmerized by the influence and power which could be exercised at the heart of Europe during the days of the Second World War. Perhaps other people's motives would be different. Some would serve out of duty, and others because it was an obvious career move, but many more out of a desire for status, power and influence.

Paul's motives are different again from those in the normal world of ambassadors. In 2 Corinthians 5 he reveals two motives which have persuaded him to serve, literally, 'for God's sake' (v. 13). The first is the fear of the Lord (v. 11) and the second is the love of Christ (v. 14).

The fear of the Lord

'Since, then,' he writes, 'we know what it is to fear the Lord, we try to persuade people' of the gospel (v. 11). The fear of which he was speaking was more than the fear spoken of in the wisdom tradition of Israel (Prov. 1:7, 29; 2:5; 3:7; 8:13; 9:10). That fear was a sense of respect and submission which arose from one's appreciation of creatureliness and finiteness before a sovereign, wise and moral creator. Paul's fear of the Lord arose from a more direct source as well. He was aware that at some stage he, together with everyone else, 'must … appear before the judgment seat of Christ, that everyone may receive what is due them for the things done while in the body, whether good or bad' (v. 10). This sense of future accountability dominated Paul's horizon in ministry and, as we shall see, was one to which he frequently referred as a force that shaped him. All his actions were calibrated by the thought of judgment. The judgment seat was, as it were, Paul's true north by which he set the direction of his Christian service.

James Denney described this as 'a motive so high, and so stern in its purifying power, [that] no minister of Christ can afford to dispense with [it]'.[13] He suggested that it had a number of crucial effects on the way in which Paul conducted his ministry. It suppressed self-seeking, kept the conscience vigorous, preserved the message from degenerating into good-natured indifference, and prevented immoral compromises and superficial remedies from being offered. To these we might add that it puts the fear of human beings and our accountability to them into a proper perspective. Denney advised, 'Let us familiarise our minds, by meditation, with the fear due to Christ the judge, and a new element of power will enter into our service, making it once more urgent and more wholesome than it could otherwise be.'[14]

Fear is no longer considered a virtue in our world. People strive to be rid of fear and see it as a sign of weakness. Self-sufficiency,

independence of action and indifference to the thoughts of others
are the virtues we prize. Living in such an atmosphere, it is hard for
pastors, let alone other Christians, to have a vital sense of the fear of
God. But if our service as an ambassador is to be preserved from
downfall and to be effective in delivery, it is an attribute we must
learn to cultivate.

The love of Christ

It is characteristic of Paul that he should neatly balance his reference
to 'the fear of the Lord' with a reference to 'the love of Christ'. It is
a necessary balance. The first without the second could cause us to
serve out of a cold and cringing sense of duty. The second without
the first would be just as unbalanced and lead us to serve out of a
wishy-washy and undisciplined sense of sentimentality. The fear of
the Lord could be seen as despairingly stern unless blended with the
love of Christ. The love of Christ could be seen as insipidly
superficial unless blended with the fear of the Lord.

Paul speaks of Christ's love compelling him – again a strange
conjunction of words, since love is often assumed to be a free
emotion. Yet we know that love does compel. Many families rejoice
when, at last, the teenage son falls in love. It means that he washes
his face, sprays his body and combs his hair as never before. The
minor inconvenience of not being able to get into the bathroom
because it is always occupied by this reborn tenant is a small
inconvenience in comparison with having a relatively presentable
human being around. Love certainly does control!

So it is with the love of Christ, which affects us in this way: it
leads us to share the message of his death with those who are dying
in order that they might find life (vv. 14–21). For Paul it genuinely
was a compulsion. 'Woe to me if I do not preach the gospel!' (1 Cor.
9:16). But it was a compulsion of love.

Paul speaks of Christ's love not only as a controlling force but as
a proven fact and a transforming power. The love of Christ was not
a matter of fantasy on his part, as it might be with a teenage
romance. It was a love which had expressed itself in the ultimate
way. It was proven by the way in which Christ gave himself for Paul,
and for us, on the cross. Christ's death means there need be no

uncertainty about the extent or absoluteness of his love. The cross makes it both incontestable and unequivocal. No wonder love like that provokes a response.

The transforming power of that love is also what sustained Paul as he occupied an alien land as an ambassador of Christ. It changes men and women. It gives their lives a new orientation. Without Christ many revolve around themselves, but his transforming love bids them come and take their directions from him (v. 15). The radically different set of values they adopt and lifestyle they begin to follow makes them new beings (v. 17). The change is not something people can bring about themselves. It is generated by God. Paul writes with utter confidence in the gospel because he had seen it to work effectively in so many lives. To him, it was 'the power of God' (Rom. 1:16) not just in theory but in fact.

These three elements of the love of Christ – its compelling force, its convincing proof and its transforming power – continue to be vital incentives to present-day ambassadors of the gospel working in equally inhospitable and alien environments. The wonder of such love is so immense that it should engender in us the spirit of C. T. Studd in his famous remark, 'If Jesus Christ be God and died for me, no sacrifice can be too great for me to make for him.'

The message of the ambassador

As Paul uses the image, the stress falls on the message, not the messenger. By referring to himself as Christ's ambassador, he is wishing to draw attention not to himself but rather to the appeal he is commissioned to convey. In Gunther Bornkamm's words, 'An important point here is that the interest of the statement (in verse 20) is focused on the (material) authority of the message rather than the (formal) authority of an officer.'[15]

It is not quite true to say that the message is everything and the messenger nothing. That is to denigrate God's creative purpose, elective choice and transforming energy. We understand what is meant by the ardent prayer, 'Thank you for sending your servant to us today. Now, Lord, blot him out that we might see Jesus only.' But whether it is theologically accurate is another matter. God created us as the summit of his creation, and, therefore, we are not 'nothing'.

His way of working has always been to choose from among the people he created those who would be particular instruments of his will or mouthpieces for his word. He could presumably have bypassed human beings, but instead he chooses to use them as his servants. In Paul's case, we see the way in which God takes up and uses all the gifts he placed in him at birth and through the socializing process which went on before conversion, as well as his particular personality, and transforms them by his Spirit so that Paul is uniquely equipped to be the apostle to the Gentiles. We see the way in which God has a craftsman's ability to shape and refashion a life so that someone can be a fitting instrument in his service. So let's not devalue the messenger altogether.

Its source

And yet, the recognition that the essential focus is on the message is important. It reminds us that ambassadors have no authority, role or dignity in themselves. The authority of their office lies in the message which is given them by God. The message has a divine source. It is not a message ambassadors have to invent, nor is it one they convey selectively to suit their own purposes. Ambassadors are charged with passing on a predetermined message unaltered. It is their responsibility to know when and how to convey it so that it will communicate effectively. But they are not to change it. It is just here that many ambassadors have mistaken their charge or gone beyond their brief. Sometimes, in a well-meaning attempt to communicate the message, the message has been adapted beyond all recognition. Sometimes they have taken upon themselves the responsibility of writing a new message. Sometimes they have been too fearful to pass it on, thinking that they lack the personal authority necessary to do so. Sidney Greidanus puts the point well:

> The only proper authority for preaching is divine authority – the authority of God's heralds, his ambassadors, his agents. Heralds and ambassadors do not speak their own word but that of their sender. Contemporary preachers, similarly, if they wish to speak with divine authority, must not speak their own word but that of their Sender.

Accordingly, if preachers wish to preach with divine authority they must proclaim the message of the inspired Scriptures, for the Scriptures alone are the word of God written; the Scriptures alone have divine authority. If preachers wish to preach with divine authority, they must submit themselves, their thoughts and opinions, to the Scriptures and echo the word of God. Preachers are literally to be *ministers* of the word.[16]

Its content

Paul dwells on the content of the message. The chief theme of the gospel, as he sets it forth here in verses 15–19, is the theme of reconciliation.[17] A holy God longs to relate to the people he has made, but there is an obstacle in the way. The obstacle is our sin, which is not only the underlying cause of all our ills (whether they be personal, relational, social, economic, political, environmental or cosmic), but also a barrier to our friendship with him. A holy God cannot coexist with a sinful people unless something is done about the sin factor. The marvel of reconciliation is that God took the initiative in seeking to remove the obstacle and the resulting alienation between us and restores our relationship with him. 'God was reconciling the world to himself in Christ' (v. 19).

The barrier was overcome through the death of Christ. The solution lay in a great exchange between us and Christ: our sinfulness for his sinlessness; our unrighteousness for his righteousness; our liability for his asset; our deadness for his life.

The reconciliation which takes place is real, and not a mere legal fiction or book transaction. It is not a peace treaty which might stitch things together on the surface without fundamentally changing the real nature of things. This reconciliation changes us completely (v. 17). We become new people and so are enabled to live within this new reconciled state. We assume a new purpose – living for God (v. 15). We acquire a new ministry (v. 18). We experience a new forgiveness (v. 19). We accept a new responsibility (vv. 19–20). We covet a new righteousness (v. 21).

In other words, the content of our message is to be what God has done for us in Christ; the Christ who was crucified (1 Cor. 1:23).

Temptations abound to preach about other things. But unless we preach Christ, we really have nothing to offer, and we are certainly not conveying the message we were sent to deliver. We are, in fact, betraying our calling and selling out to other powers. The challenge all ambassadors face must be to ask themselves regularly, 'How faithfully am I preaching Christ crucified?'

Maybe we should keep the initials 'PC' boldly in front of us as a reminder to 'Preach Christ'. Donald Messer[18] tells the amusing story of the farmer who saw the letters 'PC' in the sky and took it as a sign that he was called to be ordained. He interpreted it as 'Preach Christ'. After failing in ministry, he realized that what it actually meant was 'Plough Corn'. Messer comments, 'Today God calls persons not only to "preach Christ" but to "programme computers" and to "professional counselling."' More latterly some have felt called to 'political correctness'. I agree that all believers should feel the call of God to their work, and that the sacred/secular divide is a false one. But pastors should be clear that as ambassadors for the gospel they are called to 'preach Christ' and not to engage in whatever other activities might be implied by the initials 'PC'.

Preaching Christ is more than making a dispassionate announcement for hearers to take or leave as they like. Paul uses the language of persuasion throughout this passage. The tone of the whole passage is one of appeal, but verses 11 and 20 make the persuasive element explicit. It matters to him whether they grasp what he is saying and accept the reconciling hand which God holds out to them. It matters so much, in fact, that he will make a fool of himself if it increases the chances of his getting through to them (v. 13). True ambassadors cannot be indifferent to the response they receive. They must convey the message in the most compelling form possible, providing only that the persuasion is consistent with the integrity both of the message and of the hearers (see 2 Cor. 4:2).

Ambassadors, then, are called upon both to set out the truth *and* to let people know how they can make it their own. Donald English helpfully points out that many preachers do only one and not the other.

There is a kind of preacher whose theological weight is such that the hearers are constantly told about the wonderful banquet, but never invited to the table or told how to get there. There is another kind that constantly and urgently invites you to the table and tells the hearers how to come, without giving any sense that what is on the table is worth the journey! Our hearers need a theological content that whets their appetite, and a faith content that enables them to enter fully into all that God can be in their lives.[19]

Let every ambassador, then, be true to his or her sovereign's message and to its urgency. Let every ambassador announce the truth, but equally tell people how to make it their own. Reconciliation is already completed in the atonement, and to be completed as people respond to the invitation of the cross.

The scope of the ambassador

Normally, ambassadors have a message for governments and report only to the appropriate offices of state. But, as Christ's ambassadors, we have a message which is 'for all'. Three times, in verses 14 and 15, Paul uses the word 'all'. In verse 17 he talks of 'anyone' and in verse 19 of 'the world'. There is an inclusiveness about the gospel that Paul is concerned to emphasize alongside the awareness that not all will accept the good news. But the fact that they may not accept it should not deter the ambassador from passing it on.

One of the biggest limitations of contemporary ministry is the local church's desire to turn their pastor into a chaplain for some private religious club – a club, to boot, which is fussy about who it admits to membership. But true pastors, if they are to fulfil their ambassadorial functions, will have to overcome such misunderstanding, break out of the narrow confines of the church and transmit the message of 'God in Christ' more broadly.

The church often unconsciously operates on a basis of self-selection. It would never admit that such a policy existed, but, in practice, it passes potential converts through a filter of respectability to screen out those who are unlikely to make it or who won't fit socially with the existing members of the club. It is, after all, only efficient to do so. Since our time and resources, especially those of the paid minister, are limited, we cannot waste them. We have to ensure that they will be used where there is an economic return on the investment. So we don't mind the pastor spending a little time on the fringes of the church among promising people, providing they are just like us. But he or she must never stray too far from those who are existing members of the club, to work among those who are never likely to become members of our church.

The true role of Christ's ambassador, as set forth by Paul, brings us up with a jolt. The place of ambassadors is not among the comfortable court circles of their home territory, but in alien territory. They serve where the customs and the language are foreign. It is their task to persuade people in strange and unfamiliar dominions of their sender's message. The image, then, should cause us to reassess the way we expect our pastors to function, and how much of our time, as pastors, we spend comforting the insider and how much we engage with the outsider.

If we are ambassadors of Christ, we shall seek to imitate his style of ministry. He spent his time, not with the respectable and religious insiders, but with the outcasts and religious rejects of his day; with those whom we would often consider to be unworthy of our time because they did not seem promising material for conversion or church membership. We know, however, that surprisingly they did make the most wonderful of converts. Their lives displayed the grace and mercy of God in a way in which the religious establishment would never do. As John Wesley commented following a prison mission, 'Here is comfort, high as the heaven, stronger than death! What! Mercy for all? For Zacchaeus, a public robber? For Mary Magdalene, a common harlot? Methinks I hear one say, "Then I, even I, may hope for mercy."'[20]

Donald English[21] writes of Rembrandt's picture, *The Nightwatch*, which can be seen in the Rijks Museum in Amsterdam. It was once, he says, larger than it is today, but the authorities in Amsterdam decided it would look good between two doors in the Town Hall. They then discovered it was too big to fit there, and so chose to resolve their dilemma by cutting it down to size. As a result, three people from the original picture have been cut out. That is often what we are in danger of doing with the gospel. But Paul's image of the ambassador should forever remind us of the 'wideness in God's mercy', and that 'anyone' who is in Christ can become a new creation. Ambassadors of Christ must be inclusive in their style and reach out to all with the good news. The good news is for them, and the most unexpected people respond to it.

Conclusion

The United Kingdom hosts some 17,000 ambassadors at the present time. It has over twice that number in ordained ministry, and many more besides whose calling is to be ambassadors for Christ. Ambassadors for Christ may never be accorded the status of other diplomats. Indeed, it might be injurious to their cause if they were, since the one they assist, though Lord of all, was a suffering servant. They can, however, partake of his authority if they speak his message with faithfulness, conviction and authenticity. Motivated by both fear of him and love for him, they can be sustained in their work in what must always remain for them foreign territory. They must never sell out to it or its values. The task is not so difficult to sustain, for the message they bring is wonderfully effective in its transforming power. Seeing lives change provides constant impetus to ministry. Unlike that of other diplomats, their message is 'for all' and is to be broadcast widely. And, unlike that of others, their message is one and unchanging. It is Christ crucified.

No better summary of the role of the ambassador can be found than that given by Bishop Lightfoot in an ordination address. 'What ideas are involved', he asked, 'in this image of an ambassador?' He answered his own question in this way:

> We may sum up this conception, I think, in three words, *commission, representation, diplomacy.* The ambassador, before acting, receives a commission from the power for whom he acts. The ambassador, while acting, acts not only as an agent but as a representative of his sovereign. Lastly, the ambassador's duty is not merely to deliver a definite message, to carry out a definite policy: but he is obliged to watch opportunities, to study characters, to cast about for expedients, so that he may place it before his hearers in its most attractive form. He is a diplomatist.[22]

Questions for reflection

1. What do I think is happening when I preach? Do I have any sense of it as God working and speaking through me? If not, should I not seek a fresh filling of the Spirit for this aspect of my ministry?

2. On what do I rely to lend me dignity in the ministry? Title, dress, office, pulpit, training, or 'chains'?

3. What place does the fear of the Lord have in my ministry?

4. Am I guilty of having 'gone native' and selling out to the alien values of the territory where I am an ambassador for Christ?

5. Do I really believe in the power of the gospel and its ability to effect change in people?

6. As I examine my message, to what extent am I a person of one theme, that of Christ crucified?

7. Have I fallen into the trap of becoming the chaplain to a private religious club? How far am I imitating Jesus in reaching out to 'outsiders' with the gospel?

2
Athlete

'I do not run like someone
running aimlessly' (1 Cor. 9:26).

My school reports were always quite favourable until it came to
sport. The best I ever achieved in that area was a comment like, 'He
tries hard.' It would have given me great pleasure, though left me a
lot poorer, if I had been able to enter into the sort of arrangement
Charles Swindoll saw on offer in an advertisement for a 'rent-a-
jogger:'

> Rent me for $1.95 and I will jog for you at least one mile
> each day (weather permitting) for the next year. The
> customer will receive a suitably framed certificate, attesting
> that 'your jogger is securing for you the benefits of a healthful
> glow, extraordinary stamina, an exciting muscle tone, and a
> powerful sense of total well-being.'

'Rent-a-jogger', Swindoll adds, 'was the idea of a 45 year old
stockbroker. Within several days of the advertisement appearing,
322 people had sent him $1.95, which more than paid for it.'[1]
Unfortunately for me, the model of the athlete is one to which
Paul frequently refers when discussing the work of the ministry. It is

a rich image, capable of both extensive and sundry applications to the pastoral role. So what I never attained to on the athletics field I must strive towards in pastoral ministry. For pastors, the call to be an athlete is inescapable.

Athletic imagery in the ancient world

The Jews were not enthusiasts for games, and little reference is made in the Old Testament to anything of the sort. Jacob 'wrestled' (Gen. 32:24), and running is mentioned both literally and metaphorically (for example, Jer. 12:5), but none of these allusions contains the idea of an athletic contest. Similarly, crowns are mentioned. But they are crowns that belong to royal heads or are worn on festive occasions. Again, there is no idea in the Old Testament of a crown as a prize for winning a race. Games and athletic contests were not part of Jewish culture.

It is only later, with the onset of Hellenistic influences in the intertestamental period, that athletic imagery comes into play. When it does, as in 4 Maccabees, it is immediately used in the wider Greek sense to allude to the struggle required to create a virtuous life, of endurance and of discipline through suffering. Antiochus Epiphanes had introduced athletic contests and built gymnasia as a means of corrupting the Jews with Greek ideas, but it was Herod the Great who did most to perpetrate these foreign practices. He built lavish theatres, gymnasia and stadia in Caesarea, Jerusalem and in other Palestinian cities, and introduced quinquennial games, dedicated to the name of Caesar. The games were run in a luxurious fashion in the hope of attracting people from all over the world as competitors.

Far from reconciling his subjects to such practices, Herod found that the Jews remained suspicious of them. They saw them as foreign and contrary to their traditions, and they were irked by their extravagance. Four reasons in particular have been suggested for their opposition. First, these practices were dedicated to Caesar. Second, athletes performed in those days naked. Third, the gladiatorial contests exhibited great cruelty. And fourth, the splendid prizes and trophies which Herod distributed consisted of images which were forbidden by Jewish law.[2]

Paul, however, was a citizen of Rome and had been educated in Tarsus. In spite of his prestigious Jewish pedigree, therefore, athletics and other types of games were very much part of his cultural world. It is possible that he, at least, visited the Isthmian games, celebrated in the spring of AD 51, during one of his visits to Corinth; and he would have been familiar with the Olympic and other pan-Hellenic games as well. So it is natural for him to make frequent allusions to the world of sport in his letters, especially to running and boxing.

By Paul's time, the athletic imagery had been developed widely by Greek philosophers as a motif for striving for moral excellence as well as physical prowess. The gymnasia were centres of both physical and intellectual training. The ideal for which they strove was 'a developed mind in a body which has reached its maximum degree of perfection'. This education was based on the premise that 'everything was to be reached through training and exercise, through the maximum development of the individual with his innate latent powers'.[3]

Plato shunned the competitive element in games, but used the image to speak of the development of the soul towards a vision of the eternal ideas of righteousness, justice, temperance and knowledge. Aristotle, too, used the imagery frequently to foster a life of good fortune in which reason guided passions and impulses. It spoke for him, too, of the importance of a goal and of perseverance, especially in the face of suffering.[4]

With the Stoics and Cynics, many of these high ideals were lost and lesser understandings substituted. They saw the whole of life as a 'struggle', and set out the ideal response towards which people should work as that of impassibility. Like boxers, people should show unflinching courage in the face of opposition, welcome hardship as a sparring partner and derive strength from every victory so that they had the confidence to meet and conquer fresh opponents. Although, they conceded, such a contest was not for everyone, those who entered it should not give in or give up. Once begun, the contestant must constantly discipline himself and endure to the end.[5]

The Jewish writer Philo continued this tradition, exalting the moral athlete in contrast to the physical athlete, and applying it to the Old Testament. So Abraham becomes an example of learned virtue, and the wilderness wandering a period of great struggle towards the goal of the promised land. Unlike his Greek counterparts, Philo places a much greater stress on God's role in it all. The ideal is to be a fighter for God, and the goal of all ethical behaviour is to live for God alone. God has prepared the arena of life in which the contest takes place, and he is the one who awards the prizes.[6]

It is this common image which Paul takes up and uses to his own ends to describe both the Christian life generally and the work of the Christian pastor in particular. In doing so, he revises the images and leaves behind much that would otherwise be inconsistent with his wider theology. The Greeks, for example, assume that the goal is obtained by self-assertion and that the contestant had within him all that was needed to reach the goal after suitable training and discipline. Such a thought is foreign to Paul. The goal is not self-perfection but maturity in Christ (Col. 1:28–29). Even where his use of the image comes close to that of the wider Greek use, he still stamps his own distinctiveness on it as a God-intoxicated man.

How then does Paul use the image?

Paul employs a wide variety of the vocabulary associated with running, boxing, toiling, striving and contesting as a general metaphor of the Christian life. We might note the following as typical of his approach. The whole of the Christian experience is one of struggle and opposition (Phil. 1:27–29; 1 Thess. 2:2). The Galatians were running a good race until someone tripped them up (Gal. 5:7). Epaphras 'is always wrestling in prayer' (Col. 4:12). But the image comes into play most when he applies it to his own work. Four particular features can then be discerned.

The discipline of training

'Everyone who competes in the games goes into strict training' (1 Cor. 9:25). Paul was right. Those who entered the ancient games were not permitted to be casual contestants who made up their mind at the last moment whether or not they would compete. The games demanded very high standards, not least because they were dedicated to the Emperor or to one or more of the gods. Conscientious effort and commitment had to be demonstrated, and one way of doing that was to undergo strict training. A commitment to training was spelled out in the rules which had to be observed, mentioned by Paul in 2 Timothy 2:5. J. N. D. Kelly comments that as far as the Olympic Games were concerned, this required competitors to swear an oath before the statue of Zeus that they had been in strict training for ten months prior to their commencement.[7]

Training involved more than what an athlete did in the gym or on the track. Then, as now, it involved a commitment to a totally disciplined lifestyle. Fitness of body was acquired as much by how one lived off the track as on it, or out of the ring as in it. John Chrysostom, preaching on 2 Timothy 2, stated it like this: 'It is not enough that he enters into the lists, that he is anointed, and even engages, unless he comply with all the laws of the exercise, with respect to diet, to temperance, to sobriety and all the rules of the wrestling school, unless, in short, he go through all that is befitting for a wrestler.'[8]

It is trite to say that no contemporary athlete would dare to enter any athletic competition without having undergone strict training for the event; but it is none the less true. It is also true that the training required is as comprehensive now as then. No athlete would be concerned only about what they do in the event, as if that could be divorced from what they do elsewhere in their lives. Unhealthy eating, over-drinking and lack of sleep would soon put paid to one's chances of winning. The strict regimes imposed on teams coming up to the big match are well known. Training is designed, then, with both a positive and a negative aim in mind. Positively it seeks to develop strength, stamina and skill; negatively, it seeks to reduce the liabilities which result from unhealthy lifestyles or over-indulgent eating habits.

So it must be with the pastor and other church leaders. Training is required if the task is to be accomplished with anything like success. Theological understanding and skilled craftsmanship are important, both in handling the Word of God and in dealing with the people of God. More will be said of these as we develop the image of the pilot. But we must also pay attention to the necessary training of the pastor as a person. All the theological skills in the world, all the exegetical knowledge which can be found in any library, and all the understanding of people, difficult or otherwise, that can be found in any psychology department will be futile unless accompanied by the training in character and godliness which is equally Paul's concern.

2 Timothy demonstrates this dual concern. On the one hand, Timothy is to keep and guard 'the pattern of sound teaching' (1:13–14) and prove himself to be a worker who 'correctly handles the word of truth' (2:15). On the other hand, discharging his ministry is as much about how he lives as about what he teaches. He must 'flee the evil desires of youth' (2:22) and show himself to possess ability as a teacher by gently instructing opponents and avoiding quarrels, resentments, godless chatter and futile speculations (2:23–25). His teaching is to be marked by patience and care (4:2); perseverance, evangelistic zeal and an all-roundedness which shuns narrow specialisms that lead to an imbalance in instructing God's people (4:5). None of this would come easily. To develop such a godly character, Timothy would have to live the life of an athlete-in-training (2:5; see also 1 Tim. 4:7–8).

How many of us dare to take up pastoral ministry without thinking that any training is necessary? In recent days it has been too easy to slip, untrained and untested, into leadership positions. In part, this may have been a reaction to training which did not appear to deliver what the church needed. All the tests devised by church systems do not seem to have kept the unorthodox out of the pulpit or the ungodly out of leadership. And even if people knew the right things, they often seemed unable to relate to others well. Training often missed the mark, educating people in the wrong things and in the wrong way.

Research by the Murdoch Charitable Trust in the United States has shown that members of churches, pastors and seminary professors often look for quite different priorities when it comes to training, with the laity looking much more for the training of the person than for training in either skills or knowledge. The table opposite sets out the main findings in each group's order of priority.[9]

Tensions like these have led to an understandable impatience on the part of some, especially those from newer churches, who argued that mentoring and on-the-job training was the only legitimate and

	Lay	Pastors	Professors
1	Spirituality	Relational skills	Theological knowledge
2	Relational skills	Management abilities	Character
3	Character	Communication skills	Leadership skills
4	Communication skills	Spirituality	Communication skills
5	Theological knowledge	Theological knowledge	Counselling skills

biblical model. In spite of all its strengths, however, such an approach to developing leaders also has its limitations, and, especially in our present world, cannot be the total answer. Mentoring and on-the-job training can suffer from a narrowness which true education shuns. They seek to reproduce copies rather than develop originals. There is still room for training of the college variety which in a systematic way can educate someone in the richness and diversity of the Bible, our mission and our faith far beyond anything that can be learned in one local church. But the colleges must give as much attention to the development of the spiritual and personal growth of students as they do the intellectual aspect of their faith. Mentoring, close personal supervision, the encouragement of journal writing, the setting aside of time for worship, quiet days or retreats, and training in Christian morality, prayer, Bible memorization and faith development are all essential. And I believe the best colleges are doing just that today, whatever they have done in the past.

Besides the need for initial training and orientation – the building in of disciplines that will shape life-long ministry – the image of the athlete also reminds us that there is the need for on-going, in-service training. No athlete who did not continually train and maintain his or her body to the peak of fitness would be taken seriously. Training is not something which can be completed by the time one leaves school and never undertaken again. Success depends on maintaining fitness. Lack of up-to-date training spells ruin. The flab would soon show. Indeed, athletes who fail to train quickly go to seed and become liabilities both to their team and to themselves; their own bodies suffer as a result of a lack of recent preparation.

How different is the attitude of many pastors to on-going training? It is a common joke among pastors that you can tell when they left college by looking at the books on their shelves. They haven't bought another one since graduating. That may be over-stating the case, but there is some truth in it. Popular books concerning the latest fashion in ministry or mission are widely read, and conferences are well-attended. But much of it falls very short of serious training. On-going training of the spirit, perhaps through a commitment to a spiritual director, cell group or soul-mate; on-going working at God's Word, in depth, perhaps with the help of some recent serious books or study conferences; occasional re-tooling of one's ministry when one moves to a new church or different type of area; and continuous grappling with the place of the church in contemporary culture are all vital if ministry is to remain fresh and effective.

I confess that one of the things I have struggled with most in ministry is attending ministers' fraternals dominated by delightful but retired ministers who hijack the discussion by telling us what it was like before the 1950s. I honour their ministry, but many show no awareness of changing sociological patterns and spiritual needs. Ministry is all too easy for them. They know how to do it. They lack the sprinter Linford Christie's wisdom. 'My motto', he said, 'is never train as a champion but always as a competitor.'[10] Champion though he was, he never took anything for granted and trained regularly with humility and painstaking care. Oh that today's pastors might be baptized with such an attitude! Indifference and lack of up-to-date training show. It is easy to understand why many struggle in ministry. They've abandoned the discipline of training.

Training is a discipline that requires self-renunciation. Behind the successful athlete lie hours of sweat and pain in the gym, or on the track or the field. Behind the successful swimmer lie hours, often early in the morning while the rest of us are still in bed, in the pool. Training is not easy and the rewards are not always immediately apparent. Paul was aware that training was a discipline. He spoke of it graphically in terms of beating his body and making it his slave (1 Cor. 9:27). Our addiction to the culture of comfort means that we often flunk out of the training session because we regard it as too demanding. We would rather go in for short-term activism than submit to a costly training regime which will produce better long-term results. We think we cannot afford the time out to reflect in depth on ministry, to attend a spiritual retreat. Or we think we cannot afford to grapple with a deeper book in place of the short paperback which has direct relevance to next Sunday's sermon. We are like the person mentioned in Ecclesiastes 10:10, who expends enormous energy chopping down a tree with a blunt axe. If only he would stop chopping and sharpen the axe he would find the job a lot easier! The lesson the teacher draws from this absurd picture is that 'skill will bring success'. Training requires all sorts of investments, in time, money and sacrifice, which few are prepared to pay. Is it then surprising that many who are initially successful in the sprint lack the stamina to continue in the race? Is it any surprise that our ministries are shallow and often unproductive? Learning, reflecting, listening, reading, praying and fasting are disciplines which cost. But training brings great rewards.

The experience of struggling

The Greek word which is central to the athletic image is *agōn* (contest), from which we get our word 'agony'. Struggle, striving, effort, lie at the heart of any sporting achievement. The Greeks, as we have seen, saw life generally as a struggle. For Paul the struggle was more particular. It was a struggle for the faith: a struggle that had at least three aspects to it.

First, the exertion required to win people to the faith was a struggle. He 'contends', side by side with others, 'in the cause of the gospel' (see Phil. 4:3). Paul's extended use of the athletic imagery, in 1 Corinthians 9:24–27, arises from his discussion about winning people for Jesus Christ. In the preceding verses, 19–23, he has set out his basic missionary philosophy. Although he comes from a particular cultural background and has his own personal commitments, he leaves these comfort zones behind for the sake of the gospel, and enters the alien world of other people's subcultures. He becomes 'all things to all people so that by all possible means I might save some' (v. 23). It must have been very difficult for an educated Jew who had been liberated by the gospel of Jesus Christ to enter the worlds of those still imprisoned by the law, those who had profligate Gentile backgrounds, those who were slaves and those who were weak. But he will not be distracted from his goal, in spite of the struggle which is involved. He needs to undergo strict training in order to be effective and to keep himself on track. Without it, not only might he fail, but he might be sucked into any of those subcultural worlds and be disqualified from the race.

Paul does not make out that evangelism is easy. Far from it. It *is* a struggle. Still, today, for all the methods, techniques and resources on offer, true evangelism that engages with love in real relationships, as Paul did, will be a struggle. It will take us out of our church buildings, where we're at home, so that we can enter the world of the pubs, the sports clubs, the streets and the places where others feel at home so that we can love them for Jesus. It will demand entering what for many of us is foreign territory, where some may feel we're in danger of being contaminated. But that's part of the struggle, part of the cost we pay.

Secondly, the effort required to produce maturity of faith in those who were won for Christ was a struggle. In Colossians 1:28–29 Paul reveals his philosophy of ministry to the believers. His aim is to 'present everyone perfect in Christ'. While Paul knew the joy of ministry, with the reward of seeing progress in the believer and the depth of loving relationship which can be experienced between pastor and people, what was uppermost in his mind here was the struggle of ministry. The 'struggle' arose, in fact, out of his care and love for them (Col. 2:1–2), without which he might have been indifferent to their progress.

The goal of maturity was one which he laboured to achieve, 'struggling with all his energy, which so powerfully works in me'. It is true that, in contrast to wider Greek attitudes, Paul did not believe he had to cater for the struggle out of his own inner resources. The Holy Spirit provided the energy needed for the fight.[11] But that did not dilute the fact that ministry was a struggle. His relationship with most of the early churches is demonstration enough of the fact. Far from making smooth progress towards the goal of maturity in Christ, many early believers were being tripped up by false teaching (as in Colossians), thrown off track by legalism (as in Galatians), injured by persecution (as in Philippians or Thessalonians) or simply not getting off the starting blocks because they were failing to grasp the meaning of the gospel (as in Corinthians). Their progress was often tardy and disappointing. But Paul never lost focus, and keeping his eye on the goal kept him going through the struggle. The effort would one day prove worth it.

We underestimate the struggle involved in producing people mature in Christ at our peril. We shall soon be disappointed if we think the path to producing maturity is easy. My ministry, like everyone's if we are honest, is strewn with those who were doing well but then fell into gross sin or just became spiritually negligent. Some have been gloriously converted from atrocious backgrounds and seemed to be doing so well in the early stages, only to have problems from their backgrounds overwhelm them. The struggle is one of keeping faith, of always hoping, of never giving up in prayer, of persevering and of still being available when we've been let down. All that, of course, has to be balanced by the encouragements of those we have known where the investment of patient care and teaching has paid off and progress towards maturity is evident.

Thirdly, Paul engaged in a continuous struggle against opposition and error. That was often the cause of the lack of progress in believers. Here the image comes very close to that of the soldier, and takes on almost military significance. Indeed, in 2 Timothy 2:3–5, Paul makes a very natural transition between one image and the other.

Acts illustrates the variety of opposition Paul faced in preaching the gospel. Insulted in Philippi (Acts 16:16–40); mocked in Athens (Acts 17:16–33); attacked in Ephesus (Acts 19:23–41) and slandered in Jerusalem (Acts 21:27–36) – it was what one should expect if one was to preach a message about a crucified messiah. Conflict would always be characteristic of Christian mission and ministry.

Conflict arose not merely from the unthinking actions of human beings, expressing the knee-jerk reactions of their prejudices, but also as a result of their established mindsets (2 Cor. 10:5).

Philosophies and thought patterns would be in opposition to the gospel, and anyone wishing to engage in successful warfare for the gospel would have to counter them as well. Even more serious is the fact that the opposition stems from non-human sources, 'the powers of this dark world and ... the spiritual forces of evil in the heavenly realms' (Eph. 6:12). And yet, while the conflict would be fierce, there were resources available which would both provide protection and lead to victory (Eph. 6:13–18).

The experience of conflict in ministry is, therefore, not a sign of personal failure or inadequacy but a sign of the wider cosmic struggle between God and his opponents. Pastors who are true to the gospel and to their calling will find themselves drawn into the conflict and will inevitably experience ministry as struggle, whether because of a commitment to evangelism or a desire to see spiritual growth in believers, or by standing firm for the gospel.

The necessity of persevering

David Bennett captures the point when he says, 'One of Paul's favourite images for a ministry completed is the image of finishing a race, *not dropping out from exhaustion or getting disqualified along the way*' (italics mine).[12] Paul expresses this concern in a number of places. He commented with sadness that the Galatians 'were running a good race. Who cut in on you and kept you from obeying the truth?' (Gal. 5:7). He feared that he himself might not make the finishing line, but, for whatever reason, be disqualified from the race (1 Cor. 9:27). Towards the end of his life his judgment on his own ministry was gratifyingly summed up by his saying, 'I have fought the good fight, I have finished the race, I have kept the faith' (2 Tim. 4:7).

Not all would merit such a verdict. The pastoral epistles make us painfully aware that not all who began the race continued to the finishing line. Hymenaeus and Alexander, together with others, had 'shipwrecked their faith' (1 Tim. 1:19). Phygelus and Hermogenes had deserted Paul, and so presumably the Lord, along with 'everyone in the province of Asia' (2 Tim. 1:15). Still others had failed to complete the course. Wrong ambition, unwillingness to pay the cost, discouragement, deviant teaching and moral weakness were among the causes responsible for failure to persevere in the New Testament, and can still be identified as causes of failure in ministry today.

Ministry departments and bishops' offices must often appear more like pathology laboratories in hospitals than maternity wards. Instead of rejoicing over the birth of vibrant life into ministry, they spend their time picking over the specimens of sickness to discover the cause of disease. On many occasions there is nothing very surprising about it. Failure to take wise precautions has led to exhaustion in ministry. The energy levels get so depleted that the spiritual and personal reserves, needed to continue to give out to people and to resist temptation, have been drained away. There is no strength or resistance left, so tragedy overtakes the runner and another leader bites the dust.

Sometimes the pastoral fatality is caused by a direct attack of Satan. But more usually Satan does not need to reveal his hand so obviously. Failure to be honest about human weaknesses, failure to observe basic rules of health and relaxation, or failure to comply with simple rules about counselling (with the result, for example, that one gets too close to or involved with a needy person of the opposite sex)[13] is often sufficient to cause the unfortunate incident that prevents someone from completing the course.

Ministry is full of potential pitfalls. Some of them are integral to the work. They arise neither out of personal failure nor as a result of direct satanic attack. Working with human beings, albeit redeemed human beings, brings its fair share of discouragements, setbacks, difficulties and pressures. Sometimes these trip us up. The answer, when they do, is to pick ourselves up, learn from the experience (often with the help of a wiser and more mature trainer with whom we can be totally honest and whom we can trust to give us support and advice), and get back in the race. More often, we do not fall on our faces (we feel like resigning but don't quite do it); we stumble for a moment. The answer then is to do what we must (again, often with the help of a fellow traveller) to recover our balance and keep going.

In a high moment of tragedy in the women's 3000 metre race in the 1984 Los Angeles Olympics, Mary Decker tripped over Zola Budd's heel and was knocked out of the race. She lay writhing in agony on the track. The months of training, the high aspirations and the brilliant achievements to date came to nothing as she grovelled on the ground. It is much more tragic when a pastoral athlete fails to complete the course, for whatever reason. The degree of tragedy is much greater both because of the nature of the race and because the reward is so much greater. It is to that reward we now turn.

The joy of winning

Carl Lewis, six times an Olympic Gold Medal winner, says that his thoughts before a big race are pretty simple. 'I tell myself: Get out of the blocks, run your race, stay relaxed. If you run your race, you'll win. Just run your race. Channel your energy. Focus.'[14] He describes his 100 metre race with Ben Johnson at the 1984 Olympics, on the outcome of which hung the title of 'the world's fastest human'. Just before the race he was almost thrown by two things. First, he looked in Johnson's eyes and knew, from their colour, that he was taking steroids. Secondly, the one person he most wanted to be in the crowd, his father, had recently died. But the same method he had used over and over again worked. 'Forget the fans, I said to myself. Just run your race. I had to tell myself over and over: Focus, run your race.'[15] Johnson was apparently the winner, but was subsequently disqualified for drug abuse. Lewis always had been the real winner, and eventually was awarded the gold medal. The secret lay in the one word, 'focus'.

What kept Paul going, throughout his ministry, was his focus on the goal. It was the thought of reaching the finishing tape and of what he would receive when he did. The goal was all-important and nothing was going to distract him from achieving it. How easily distractions come, and how hard they are to resist! All parents who have watched their child running well at a school sports day know how easy it is for the race to be won one moment and lost the next because of distraction. The distraction may be the cheering of the crowd,[16] or the momentary sideways glance at the competitors. Either way, taking one's eyes off the finishing tape often means the race is lost.

The distractions in ministry are legion. Popularity can make us water down the message, seek further glory for ourselves and assume the place that God alone should have. Hardships can make us look elsewhere and desire to serve in another church which we believe to be more promising, or in another occupation which will pay better with less hassle. Legitimate issues, doctrines or experiences can assume an importance they do not deserve, so that we become pastors who ride hobby-horses rather than declare the whole counsel of God. Failures, either our own or those of others, can hinder us.

Paul was determined not to take his eye off the tape. He focused on the reward. He was running for the 'crown that will last for ever' (1 Cor. 9:25). He was determined to 'press on towards the goal to win the prize for which God has called me heavenwards in Christ Jesus' (Phil. 3:14).

What exactly was the prize? In Philippians 4:1 and 1 Thessalonians 2:19 he states that his converts are his crown. His delight and reward lie in displaying them as evidence of work well done. 'It may be taken for granted', Howard Marshall comments, 'that Paul is not looking forward here to any sort of proud display of his apostolic achievements before the Lord Jesus, but is rather thinking of the joyful exultation which he will be able to feel when the work which God has done through him is recognised.'[17] If his crown is made up of the believers he has seen won to Christ, the prize can surely be nothing other than seeing them brought, at last, to perfection in Christ by the final transforming power of the Holy Spirit. The crown is a reward in the sense that God crowns Paul's faithfulness and endurance in his calling as an apostle by bringing it to completion.[18] What a thrill it will be, not only for Paul but for all faithful pastors, to know that their work is owned by God in this way and finished off to perfection by him. But the crown comes only to those who keep their eye on the goal.

The crown the athlete of faith looks forward to differs from the prizes awarded at ancient athletic contests in a number of ways. In any athletic competition, then or now, there is only one winner. Medals of gold, silver or bronze may be awarded, but, frankly, it's only the one who comes first, who gets the gold, who counts. In this race there is no need for competition. All can have prizes. We are not running against others to get the one and only reward. Somebody else's success is not the measure by which we shall be judged. We've no need to beat their record by scoring more converts or presenting ourselves and our work in a better light. Jealousy easily enters, but it is both evil and unnecessary. God rewards us according to the way we have run the race marked out for *us*, not another (Heb. 12:1; see also John 21:20–22).

Secondly, the crown differs because, although it relates to our effort and endurance, it is really a further gift of God's grace. We do not have to win it from a reluctant God who will award it only on the basis of our self-sufficient effort. In his grace he equips us for the race, enables us to win and then bestows upon us the crown.

Thirdly, the crown that we shall receive differs from prizes at earthly athletic events because it will neither perish nor tarnish. Paul makes the point vividly in 1 Corinthians 9:25. Athletes go into strict training and put in all that effort 'to get a crown that will not last'. In his day this was literally true. The athletic prize awarded at the Isthmian Games was a crown of greenery. Neither that, nor the rapturous welcome the winning contestant would receive on his return home, would last. Was it worth it? Even in our own day, the precious metal will tarnish or the thief will steal it. Records will be broken and great achievements will be forgotten. By contrast, the Christian athlete receives a crown 'that will last for ever'. That surely is worth it.

Conclusion

Effort, endurance, focus, training, discipline, determination, struggle, opposition and contest are the hallmarks of the athlete. They should mark Christian leaders no less than the literal athlete. But if they seem demanding, they are all outweighed by the goal and reward which will be received when the race is over. It is this that makes it all worth it.

Questions for reflection

1. How far should I compare my approach to ministry with the approach of an athlete? Does it relate in any way?

2. What is my attitude to training? How important is it to me? Do

I see the need for on-going training? If so, what arrangements have I made to undertake some? Or do I believe I finished my training when I left college, never to do any more?

3. What is my spiritual fitness programme like? Do I need to submit to a programme to help me fight spiritual flab?

4. To what extent do I accept that struggle will always characterize genuine Christian ministry? Do I resent it and try to deny it?

5. What are the weak points in my life that are likely to cause me to stumble and drop out of the race? What am I doing to overcome them?

6. Is the way I am practising my ministry likely to enable me to persevere? Am I going to be able to endure? If not, what can I do to change my approach and pace myself better so that I will endure to the end?

7. Have I got my eye fixed on the finishing tape? Or am I distracted by people and diversions closer to hand?

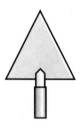

3
Builder

'... as an expert builder ...' (1 Cor. 3:10).

There is something deep within our human psyches which makes us want to build. From the Tower of Babel to the CN Tower above the Metro Centre in Toronto (currently, at 553.34 metres, the tallest free-standing structure in the world), humans have been inveterate builders. From the great temples of the ancient world – of Solomon, or of Artemis – through the magnificent cathedrals of medieval Europe to the gleaming present-day temples of commerce we have always loved to build.

National Geographic have recently celebrated great human achievements with the publication of a book called *The Builders: Marvels of Engineering*, which they describe as offering a 'compelling, close-up look at the world's most imaginative structures and the people who built them'. It includes references to the 45 tons of paint it takes to paint the 985-foot high Eiffel Tower, to the 300,000 panes of glass which composed the Crystal Palace, the 600 million tons of stone used to build the Great Pyramid, the way the Japanese are using heavy weights on the upper levels of buildings to fight earthquakes, the fact that the Empire State Building is six inches shorter today than when it was built in 1931, and the news that the Golden Gate Bridge sways as much as 28 feet in the wind. There is something to celebrate here, something intriguing and something dubious.

It is not difficult to find sinister motives for this habitual behaviour. The Bible attributes the building of Babel to the desire to reach the heavens, 'so that we may make a name for ourselves and not be scattered over the face of the whole earth' (Gen. 11:4). The same quest for godlike status, to leave monuments to themselves and to find security in bricks and mortar, has, one suspects, motivated many builders down the years, even when, as in the case of cathedrals and churches, the builders protested that they were building solely for the glory of God.

But a more positive light can be shed on our desire to build. With a mixture of plain common sense and theological profundity, Hebrews 3:4 reminds us that 'every house is built by someone, but God is the builder of everything'. God was in the construction business first, creating our universe out of nothing, and what he built was good. As men and women made in his image, it is not altogether surprising, then, that we also should wish to build. Nor is it surprising that, being marred by sin, what we wish to build should often be a shoddy shrine to ourselves rather than something more wholesome and glorifying to God.

The task of building readily lends itself to be used as a metaphor, and is especially appropriate to those called to exercise leadership in the church. The idea of building, applied, not to bricks and mortar, but to the building of communities, is a recurring biblical theme. When Paul applies the image to his apostolic calling, and so, by extension, to our pastoral responsibilities, he was not introducing a new image. Rather, he was developing a structure on the foundations already laid in the Old Testament and in the ministry of Jesus.

Early biblical use of the image

Three streams flow into the image which Paul uses. The first is that of the tabernacle and the temple. The second is that of Jeremiah and of the reconstruction of later Judaism. And the third is that of the coming of the Messiah.

The tabernacle and the temple were both buildings of sorts. But they symbolized different things. God commanded Moses to build the tabernacle and gave him careful instructions as to how it was to be done. The tabernacle was the place where God himself chose to dwell among his people (Exod. 25:8). Its setting was at the heart of the camp and its layout provided important visual aids to the people as they came to offer sacrifices. It was a beautiful structure which mirrored the majestic artistry of God the creator (Exod. 35:20 – 36:1). It was a mobile structure in line with the idea that the children of Israel were a pilgrim people who had not yet reached their destination.

In many ways the temple continued where the tabernacle left off. It was to be the dwelling place of the living God, and so needed to be worthy of him. But the temple, for all its benefits, was also something of a trap. Howard Snyder picks up one strand of the biblical witness, and contrasts the tabernacle and the temple sharply – perhaps too sharply: 'The tabernacle was God's idea; it was his design. He commanded it. But what of the temple? ... the temple was David's idea, not God's.'[1]

The motives for building the temple were tainted with elements of human pride, and the method of its building was tainted by injustice and oppression. Warning notes, advising of potential 'spiritual fault-lines' in the building of the temple, were sounded forcefully (2 Sam. 7:5–7; 2 Chr. 6:18). But the biblical record suggests they were not sufficiently heeded.

It is significant that the temple was the idea of the king. God had not desired his people to be ruled by kings, because he was their king and he knew the tendency of earthly rulers to rule despotically (1 Sam. 8:4–22). But Israel wanted to be like everyone else. Kings love building monuments, and delight even more to use the poor to do the building and to pay the taxes required to meet the bills (Eccles. 2:4–11). Partially at least, the building of the temple was an instrument of self-aggrandisement, and the account of its building in the books of Kings is fully aware of the injustice and oppression which were involved.[2]

Churchill's famous aphorism, 'We shape our buildings, then our buildings shape us', holds true here as elsewhere. The temple was a fixed structure which could not contain God. But, having built it, the people too quickly came to think that God was contained within it and no longer the sovereign, free God who was too great to live in any earthly structure. Instead, they thought of him as 'their' God, believing that they had tamed him, and that he was on their side and theirs alone. So grew the abuse of God which led, in the end, to the nation's downfall.

Of course, the temple can be seen in a more positive light, as some passages in the Bible show. It was not the temple as such that was a problem, but the people's attitudes. Yet the unfolding revelation of God's will makes it clear that the temple he desires is not built with impressive stone and overlaid with magnificent gold, but is made up of people reconciled to him and to one another by the cross of Christ (Eph. 2:11–22; 1 Pet. 2:5). The temptation is constantly to substitute the one for the other.

The second Old Testament stream flows from Jeremiah. Called to prophesy at a time when Israel had gone to seed spiritually and when the stipulations of the covenant had been broken, his was a double-edged commission to 'uproot and tear down, to destroy and overthrow, to build and to plant' (Jer. 1:10). Both demolition and reconstruction were inherent in his call. Demolishing the old and clearing the ground are often the first tasks before any new building can begin (see Neh. 4:10). So it was with Jeremiah, who witnessed the demolition of Judah from an uncomfortably near ring-side seat, but was then called to enable his fellow countrymen to rebuild their community in the new circumstances of the exile and beyond.

His focus was as much on the future of Israel, after the exile had run its course, as on the present. Through him, God, true to his essential nature as a God of grace and love, promised, 'My eyes will watch over them for their good, and I will bring them back to this land. I will build them up and not tear them down; I will plant them and not uproot them' (Jer. 24:6). Twice more, the promise of rebuilding came through Jeremiah (31:4 and 33:7). It was a vision of what the future building could be that sustained them through the dark years of decline and exile. Paul owes much to Jeremiah's use of building imagery in what he writes.

The building image became common in later Judaism as the prospect of restoration to their own land became a possibility. The rabbis spoke of building 'the house of Israel' and of the scribes as 'builders of the Torah'.[3]

The third stream has its source in the expectations of the coming Messiah. At last it was understood that because of God's greatness, human beings were not considered able to build God a house (Acts 15:16). But it was expected that the Messiah would do so (Mark 14:58).

In the mouth of Jesus the imagery becomes fluid. He warns, for example, about building life on the right foundations (Matt. 7:24–27). But, as David Peterson has pointed out,[4] the twin foci in the gospels are Christological and eschatological. That is to say that, in line with the prophecy of Psalm 118:22–23, the decisive person to bring about the new community, of which the building of a temple was a powerful symbol, was the Christ. He who was rejected at his crucifixion was the one who would build a church that could not be defeated (Matt. 16:18), form a community which was international in scope (Matt. 21:42–43), bring judgment upon those who opposed him (Matt. 21:44) and raise up a new temple which could never be destroyed (Mark 14:58). The building of this new church, then, is intimately linked to the life, death and resurrection of Jesus. It has no identity apart from him.

Given this rich and varied teaching, it was not surprising that the idea of building became a common image used to describe the growth and development of the early Christian community (for example, Acts 9:31; 20:32).

Paul's use of the image

The apostle Paul frequently turned to building imagery to describe both his own apostolic ministry and the life of the church generally. Paul's uses of the image are diverse. The gift of prophecy and other spiritual gifts are given to 'build up' the body of Christ and strengthen and encourage the church (1 Cor. 14:3–5, 12, 17, 26). God, on the one hand, gives leaders to his church who are gifted in particular ways so that they can build it up (Eph. 4:11–16), but, on the other hand, it is also the privilege and responsibility of every member of the church to build one another up (1 Thess. 5:11). Here is a ministry that all can join to everyone's mutual benefit. It is not a ministry reserved for a special few who have been either charismatically empowered or episcopally ordained. Mutual ministry, in which all the members of the body engage, however, does not detract from the calling of some to exercise authority in the church. Those who have been entrusted with authority must be very careful in their exercise of it, ensuring that they use it to build up and not tear down. It must be used to further the spiritual growth of people and the work of the gospel, not to enslave or stunt people's growth in Christ; still less to inflate the leader's ego or feed his or her lust for power (2 Cor. 10:8; 13:10). The temptation to abuse power is a subtle and ever prevalent one.

Paul, himself, was called to be a pioneer and therefore avoided working where the gospel had already been established through someone else's work. As he put it, he did not want to 'be building on someone else's foundation' (Rom. 15:20). That is not everyone's calling – but it was his.

From these verses, David Peterson summarizes the task of building. He says that it applies to the work of evangelism and church planting, but also to the process of teaching and encouragement beyond that initial task. 'It involves "founding, maintaining and advancing the congregation", as God's eschatological building'.[5] The image calls into question the mission versus maintenance debate, as if the two can be separated. The task of the pastor is both mission and maintenance. It is the pastor's calling to see the church grow both numerically and organically; both as people are added to it and as people mature within it. The builder cannot choose between the two.

It is in 1 Corinthians 3:10–17 that Paul applies the idea of the builder most fully to the work of the Christian leader. He refers to himself, presumably in his apostolic role, as 'an expert builder', but then immediately includes others, who are not apostles, in the same enterprise. The label he gives himself is that of *architektōn*, a word which is used here only in the New Testament. It means a master builder, a contractor or director of works.[6] Others also build, but their work simply supports that of the apostles. The three major emphases of his teaching apply to master builder and ordinary builder alike. You and I, then, are included.

First, Paul focuses on the process

The process starts with grace

The task of building the church of God is full of pitfalls. Chief among them is the desire, we have already noted, to build monuments to ourselves. I wonder whether that is why Paul begins his teaching in the way he does by a reference to *the grace of God* (v. 10). A friend of mine was the chief engineer on the Docklands Light Railway. Another friend was the senior engineer on the building of the massive suspension bridge which spans the islands to connect the mainland to the new airport in Hong Kong. On occasions, I have stood with architects and builders admiring their new creations of churches and colleges. All of them take a justifiable pride in their work. Their skill, qualifications and expertise are evident in the work they have accomplished. But the minister of the gospel is qualified to build only 'by the grace God has given'. No minister is eligible to build because of natural giftedness, family connections, denominational labels or theological education.

The ground of one's calling and qualification is the sheer unmerited love of God in choosing and equipping us. There are, then, no grounds for boasting. Paul returns to the same issue again and again in his letters to the Corinthians. Given their intoxication with the exercise of dramatic spiritual gifts, it is likely that the confidence of the Corinthians resided in the use of the gifts rather than in the one who gave them. So Paul reminds them that they have nothing which they did not receive from God, and, since they received it as a gift, he questions why they feel any right to boast as if the gifts were somehow their own, arising from right or natural ability (1 Cor. 4:7). Later he returns to the same point. 'Not that we are competent in ourselves to claim anything for ourselves, but our competence comes from God. He has made us competent as ministers of a new covenant ...' (2 Cor. 3:5–6).

Paul shows the Corinthians that being aware that our calling to ministry is solely grounded on the grace of God leads to the cultivation of two vital qualities. On the one hand it leads, as we have seen, to humility. Given the popularity of the success syndrome of our day, we need to have that message reinforced. Our value in ministry is secured by his grace, not our success. Awareness of the latest evangelism techniques, developments in liturgy, strategies for growth, approaches to counselling or emphases on user-friendliness may have their place. But it is God's grace that qualifies us, not our ability to master the latest ministerial fad.

Equally, on the other hand, it leads to perseverance. In a very moving passage about the struggles Paul faced as an authentic preacher of the gospel in a church full of charlatans, he states, 'since through God's mercy we have this ministry, we do not lose heart' (2 Cor. 4:1). If confidence resided in ourselves, faced as we are with pressures from both well-meaning friends and ill-meaning counter-feits, we might soon give up. But if God's grace has called us, God's grace will be adequate to resource us for all we need (Jas. 4:6) and keep us going. Indeed, since it is a calling of God's grace, we dare do no other than keep going.

The process concentrates on people

A second element of the task, to which Paul calls attention, is the nature of the building we are called to build. While some measure the achievement of their ministries by boasting of glass cathedrals, mini St Paul'ses, or efficient conference arenas, Paul is acutely conscious that it is a community, not a bricks and mortar, which he is establishing. 'You yourselves', he writes, 'are God's temple' (1 Cor. 3:16). God lives not in a stone and mortar structure but among the people; in the relationships of those who compose the church.

The idea of the church as a temple building comes naturally, given the Old Testament background. But here is a temple building which is alive, growing and developing. It is dynamic, or, better still, organic. This temple is anything but a pile of inert stones! Edmund Clowney puts it well when writing of Peter's comment that members of the church are 'living stones' and so part of a growing house (1 Pet. 2:5). Clowney pithily writes, 'God's architecture is biological.'[7]

How hard it is to keep that in view! Of course, we know it to be true and often preach on it. And yet in practice it is somehow different. Most churches find it easy to get excited when a building project is mooted. Discussion at church meetings or Parochial Church Councils will become animated when alterations are suggested, new buildings are proposed or even a fresh coat of paint is envisaged. On the whole, we find it less easy to talk excitedly about what it takes to build the community, and we are even less prepared to invest money in it than in bricks and mortar.

Building buildings takes knowledge, patience and skill. I know that I have few of the necessary qualities, as my feeble efforts at DIY bear testimony. But if bricks, cement, hammers, screws, wood and paint are difficult to handle, building a community of living people is worse. Screws, nails and tools are lifeless. They seem capable only of 'doing their own thing' when in the hands of an inexpert craftsman. But people are another matter. They really are alive and active participants, for good or ill, in the task of building.

Years ago, Derek Copley, then Principal of Moorlands Bible College, wrote a book with the delightful title *Building with Bananas*.[8] The publisher's blurb went like this:

> Why not admit it? We're all bent – more or less. So how can we fit snugly alongside each other in the fellowship of the local church? Timorous, aggressive, sluggish, hyperactive, submissive, rebellious – Christians are all these in turn – and even at the same time. Often we don't understand ourselves, let alone other people.

It was a true picture of the church and a brilliant insight into why it is so difficult to build community. But that's what the image of the leader as builder is all about.

The process involves a team

Buildings can be built single-handedly, but that is not normal! Usually, building involves a team and takes time. Paul is certainly aware, even though he calls himself an expert builder and may be the director of works, that he is one of a number of people whom God has called into the enterprise of building his church. 'I laid a foundation as an expert builder, and someone else is building on it' (1 Cor. 3:10). In the larger picture, many are involved and 'each one' must be careful how he or she builds.

Every pastor must be aware that he or she plays a limited role at one particular part of a church's story. Besides inducing humility,

once more, the insight is important for other reasons. Others will
have been before them and others are likely to follow, unless the
Lord returns first. Pastors come, most likely, into a church which
already has a story and which will have a future after them. They are
wise, then, to listen to the story so far and not to write it off as
unimportant. What has gone before will significantly shape the
perceptions, expectations, ethos and communal lifestyle of the
church. It is foolish to think that any pastor starts with a clean sheet
of paper. The failure to appreciate past history often accounts for
the initial resistance a pastor may encounter to new ways of doing
things.

Then, the pastor is part of a wider team not only as in a relay
race, where the baton is passed on from one to another, but as in a
football match where we must play with the team God has called on
to the field for the present fixture. Ideas of 'one-man ministry'
which are so ingrained in much of our church life could not be
further removed from the image of the church as set out in the New
Testament, where every member is a minister with gifts which must
be exercised if the whole body is to function and grow healthily,
even if there are some among them who have the gift of leadership.
The image militates against any concept of solo ministry.

The process takes time
The idea of a process also leads us to focus on the question of time.
The great cathedrals of the Middle Ages often took four or five
centuries to complete. Naturally this would mean that one would
lay a foundation, another would build this part, another that, and
yet others would put the finishing touches.[9] It makes me wonder
whether we are not often in too much of a hurry to accomplish the
work and need to see it in a longer-term perspective. I am grateful
for the comment which has often helped me, in my impatience, to
put things into focus. 'Remember', I was once told, 'that we usually
overestimate what can be accomplished in one year and
underestimate what can be accomplished in five.' That has proved
true in my own pastoral experience, and remembering it has saved
me from giving up too easily. There may be many periods in
ministry when we feel as if we're living in the middle of a
construction site. And so we are. The important thing is not to lay

down our tools, go absent or strike when the work has just got under way. We must keep looking forward to the day when the building will be finished and the job complete.

Several varied reflections, then, arise from the way in which Paul uses this image to speak of the task of building. But the heart of the matter is still to be reached.

Secondly, Paul focuses on the foundation

Foundations are of utmost importance to buildings, as I have good cause to know. Much of the area in which my wife and I live is afflicted with a clay soil which, unless foundations are adequate, means that buildings are liable to subsidence. Our house, built just before recent understanding ensured that such problems don't arise, suffers in a mild form from subsidence, or it did so until recent remedial action has, we hope, cured the problem. In our case, it means that cracks appear all over the house, especially as soon as we've decorated a room. Nothing too dramatic, but a pity none the less. In other cases the problem is more severe and buildings literally fall apart. Careful soil testing takes place now before any new building is put up on our college site. If there is a problem, deep piles are driven into the earth, some as tall as the building we wish to erect, to ensure that it will be built on a solid foundation. We have learned the hard way that only firm foundations give 'structural protection from the bottom up', as builders say.

The only foundation for Christian ministry is Jesus Christ (1 Cor. 3: 11). In the context of his first two chapters, it is clear that Paul only has one Christ in mind and that is Christ crucified. As Gordon Fee has written, 'The foundation is not proper doctrine, the concern of a later period, but the gospel itself, with its basic content of salvation through Jesus Christ.'[10] All would agree in theory. But what does it mean in practice?

Let's start negatively. The Corinthians, judging by the context in which this verse is found, were in danger of building their faith on the foundation of contemporary Greek wisdom rather than on Christ. There are similar faults today. It would be interesting to ask an observer, who knew nothing about the Christian faith, to look at contemporary ministry and describe what foundation it was built on. How much, I wonder, would the observer conclude that the foundation was Jesus Christ?

Several alternative foundations seem popular today. Some have made doctrines other than the cross central. Some build on the foundation of their own charismatic (with a small 'c') personality or their gift of spell-binding communication – whether they have any authentic biblical content or not. Some build on particular spiritual experience, such as being slain in the Spirit, which, even if biblical justification can be mounted for such a practice, is hardly the centre of any authentic biblical practice of ministry. Some make the foundation of their ministries a Freudian understanding of counselling or some other therapeutic school of psychology. The foundation for many in recent evangelical history has been an age-related social programme. More recently, some evangelicals have appeared to make contemporary culture the real foundation, meriting William Willimon's stricture, 'In leaning over to speak to the modern world, I fear we may have fallen in.' And it has prompted his further comment that 'The Bible doesn't want us to speak to the modern world; the Bible wants us to convert the modern world.'[11]

None of this is to say that spiritual experience is irrelevant, social programmes are to be shunned, contemporary psychological insights have nothing to contribute, evangelistic strategies are to be ignored and learning to speak to contemporary culture is unimportant. The point is that none of these things should be our foundation.

The blunt and simple challenge is to make Jesus Christ, and him crucified, alone, the foundation of all our ministry.

Paul certainly does not mean less than that. But I wonder if he means more. When applied to ministry, is not the foundation of Jesus Christ more inclusive? It is about our message plus ... In other words, we are to build on him not only by preaching his cross but also by doing ministry his way. That means we shall do the following seven things.

Love his people
There are no hidden secrets about the effectiveness of Jesus' ministry, or any missing secret we've not yet uncovered about how to reach people effectively. The simple truth is, love is what counts.

Rick Warren is right: 'The most overlooked key to growing a church: we must love unbelievers the way Jesus did.'[12] He could equally have said, 'we must love believers the way Jesus did'.

Obey his teaching

The Sermon on the Mount is simultaneously impossible and inescapable. Jesus called his followers to live their lives on a totally different basis from those around them. Building our ministries on the foundation of Jesus Christ will mean not only speaking about his cross but living according to the lifestyle he commands. Without it, our ministry will ring hollow. It will lack integrity and authenticity.

Imitate his ways

From a ministry perspective, this might well mean spending much more of our time with the marginalized people in our society, the ones who carry no status as far as 'comfortable' society or the 'respectable' church is concerned. It is commonplace to acknowledge that Jesus had most trouble with the religious people – especially religious leaders – of his day, while those who were most open to the good news were those who were written off and desperate. But how should that affect our ministry? Surely, if he is the foundation of our ministry, these people, rather than the pious insiders, ought to be the ones to whom we are giving ourselves most.

Discern his will

Jesus Christ spent time consulting with his Father, with the result that he could claim: 'I tell you the truth, the Son can do nothing by himself; he can do only what he sees his Father doing, because whatever the Father does the Son also does' (John 5:19). Too many of us spend our time finding out what others are doing and imitating them. We seek to be just like them. Far better to discern what the Father wants to do in our situation, since unless he is in it nothing will be accomplished. But discerning his will takes courage, for it might just mean that we are called to be different from other churches. Bill Hybels, the Senior Pastor of Willow Creek Community Church, in teaching about the philosophy and style of

Willow Creek, has persistently urged other church leaders not to copy their 'seeker-friendly' approach, as if merely adopting their formula will bring success. He speaks of the way in which just as every thumb-print is different, so each church leader needs to discern God's thumb-print on the church he or she leads.

Endure his cross

The cross is not only something we preach, it is something we live. We do not merely point back to it as the most critical event of history, we display it in our present-day living. Paul's own ministry was constantly marked by suffering, frustration and pain. Far from seeking to be free from these, so that he could glide from one triumph and success to another, he interpreted it as a sign of the genuineness of his ministry. He speaks of ministry without pretence as a ministry which will lead us to identify with the suffering of Christ (2 Cor. 4:7–12; 10:1 – 13:4). Only through our experience of death can life come to others.

Experience his resurrection

In tension with 'sharing in his sufferings', we are also to experience 'the power of his resurrection' (Phil. 3:10). Ministry will not be all cost. At the same time as the struggles go on, we shall also know the life-giving power of Jesus flowing through us. Victories will be won and signs of Satan's defeat will be evident. People will be converted to Christ and liberated into his kingdom of life. The Spirit's transforming power will be seen as people grow up in Christ. Prayers will be answered; healings will take place; advances will occur; arguments will be refuted and opposition will be overcome.

Proclaim his truth

All this must be integrated with the gospel we preach. If ministering on the foundation of Jesus Christ is more than speaking of him and his cross, it is nevertheless not less than speaking of the historic and biblical Christ and his cross. Unless we preach the one apostolic gospel of 'Christ and him crucified', we have nothing to offer a broken and needy world.

Thirdly, Paul focuses on the materials

All may be well with the foundations, but there remains the question of the quality of the materials to go on top. Shoddy materials, going for the cheap option, can sometimes ruin a building, no matter how good the foundations. So it is with ministry, as Paul points out.

He confronts us with a choice

There are two sorts of materials with which we can choose to build: gold, silver and costly stones, or wood, hay and straw (v. 13). The first three were used in the building of Solomon's temple; the second three are associated with traditional images of fuel for burning.[13] The former are fit for God's temple; the latter are fit only for human dwellings. The former are superior; the latter are inferior. The former endure; the latter do not last. The former are beautiful; the latter are mediocre.

D. A. Carson has set out with persuasive force what this means for us.

> This ought to be extremely sobering to all who are engaged in vocational ministry. It is possible to 'build the church' with such shoddy materials that at the last day you have nothing to show for your labour. People may come, feel 'helped,' join in corporate worship, serve on committees, teach Sunday school classes, bring their friends, enjoy 'fellowship,' raise funds, participate in counselling sessions and self-help groups, but still not really know the Lord. If the church is being built with large portions of charm, personality, easy oratory, positive thinking, managerial skills, powerful and emotional experiences, and people smarts, but without repeated passionate, Spirit-anointed proclamation of 'Jesus Christ and him crucified,' we may be winning more adherents than converts. Not for a moment am I suggesting that, say, managerial skills are unnecessary, or that basic people skills are merely optional. But the fundamental nonnegotiable, that without which the church is no longer the church, is the gospel, God's 'folly,' Jesus Christ and him crucified.[14]

He confronts us with the consequences

When a building is erected today, inspectors visit it in the course of its construction to ensure that it complies with the regulations and plans submitted. Paul's concern is not the earthly building inspector but the heavenly divine inspector. The ministries we conduct now will one day be subject to examination, and then our 'work will be shown for what it is, because the Day will bring it to light' (1 Cor. 3:13). Paul was saying that the Christians at Corinth were not in a position to judge his work.[15] Today, still, pastors are answerable to the Lord, and others are not fully in a position to evaluate our work. He, then, is both our consolation and our critic. If only we were more concerned about what the Lord will one day say than we are about other people's opinions, whether they are bishops or deacons, members or unbelievers, it would free us from much wrong pressure and give us healthier incentives in ministry. It is his voice that counts.

The method by which our work will be examined is by subjecting it to fire. Some of the edifices we have erected through our ministry will survive the test and others will be reduced to a pile of ashes. Note that it is the building which survives or suffers, not us. Our salvation is secure. To quote Carson again:

> Nothing is said about tormenting the builders and purging them in the flames. Rather, it is the quality of their work that is revealed by the fire ... The picture is of someone running out of a building engulfed in a great fire. That person escapes. But how much of the building on which he has been working survives the flames?[16]

The awful prospect is presented that when Christ finally inspects our work it will all be wasted. Paul was acutely conscious of the final day as the day when his ministry would be evaluated, and not before. He was aware of the possibility that all that he had done might have been in vain (1 Cor. 9:24–27; Phil. 2:16; 1 Thess. 2:16–17). The eschatological dimension puts everything about our ministries in their right perspective. It saves us from giving in to shorter-term goals, unworthy ambitions or human authorities. It makes us keep an eye on the Lord to whom we are answerable.

An alternative to the combustible scenario is, thankfully, also presented. It is the prospect that the materials of the building will survive the test, in which case we 'will receive a reward' (1 Cor. 3:14). The New Testament is less reticent about speaking of rewards than we sometimes are. We shy away from it, lest we degenerate into the belief that we somehow merit our place in heaven. But there is a rightful expectation that a person who has served well will receive a reward (for example, Matt. 6:4, 6, 18; 10:42; 1 Cor. 3:8; 2 John 8; Rev. 3:10–11). Here is a positive incentive to minister well. We need to keep our eye on the goal of seeing our Master and being rewarded by him.

He confronts us with a conviction
Having developed the idea of the builder and, indeed, the building team, Paul is still not done. In Corinth people had used leaders as their pawns in a game of one-upmanship and division in the church. Leaders, then, instead of being builders, had, perhaps unwittingly, become destroyers. The stones of the temple were being torn one from another. But this work of demolition had its price. God cares passionately about the unity of the church. So, 'If anyone destroys God's temple, God will destroy that person: for God's temple is sacred, and you are that temple' (1 Cor. 3:17). It cannot be too often repeated that our responsibility is to build and not to pull down.

Conclusion

Evangelists, church planters, pastors, teachers and leaders must ensure, then, that the work in which they engage is construction and not demolition. Sadly, recent days have witnessed a number of divisions in local churches because of the well-meaning and enthusiastic, but ultimately inept and culpable, leadership of some desiring to move the church forward. As we have seen in Jeremiah, it is true that demolition must sometimes precede construction. But Paul's warning in 1 Corinthians 3:17 suggests the need to be extremely sure of a call to 'tear down'. If some really are called to the exceptional ministry of demolition, they must ensure that, rather than leaving heaps of rubble around the place and allowing the church to look like a left-over bomb site, they go on to build a temple in which God himself takes up residence.

The challenge is to build – to establish, extend and augment, through evangelism, teaching and pastoral care, the temple of God's people which is currently under construction. In doing so we must pay particular attention to the foundation on which we build and the materials we use. If we do not, the building will one day be no more than a heap of dirty ash.

Questions for reflection

1. As I examine my motivation for ministry, to what extent can I truly say it is to build God's temple and not to erect a monument to myself?

2. Have I made sufficient allowances for the time the process takes, or am I too impatient to see things achieved?

3. Do I see myself as part of a team, even if I am the director of works, or am I trying to build the church on my own?

4. Is there a sense in which I am called to 'tear down' as well as 'build up?' Have I been sufficiently cautious and honest about any ministry of demolition?

5. Can I truthfully say that the foundation of my ministry is Jesus Christ and him only? What would others say was the foundation of my ministry?

6. What materials am I using to build God's temple?

7. Is my heart in building – or in just an occasional redecoration of the church?

4
Fool

'... receive me just as you
would a fool' (2 Cor. 11:16).

The word 'fool' is deceptively simple. We are familiar with it as a straightforward label for someone who lacks sense, who engages in inappropriate behaviour and suffers from a wisdom bypass. Such people are neither lovable rogues nor amusing clowns, but people who are stupid in the handling of their lives and eternal destinies. The Bible uses the word on numerous occasions in this way. Fools say, 'There is no God' (Ps. 14:1). They cannot be corrected by reason, but only by the use of a rod (Prov. 26:3). They build their houses on sand (Matt. 7:24–27), invest only in the material at the expense of the spiritual (Luke 12:13–21) and are ill-prepared for the most momentous appointment they will ever have to keep (Matt. 25:1–13).

This, however, does not exhaust the meaning of the word 'fool'. There is another, subtler, meaning which is the one Paul has in mind when he claims that he and Apollos were 'fools for Christ' while the Corinthian church members were 'so wise in Christ'. His brief claim, in 1 Corinthians 4:10, was the first sounding of an ironic note which would develop into a major theme later in his correspondence with the church in Corinth; namely in 2

Corinthians 10 – 13. There he rhapsodizes on the glory of serving Christ as a fool. Although it may not come readily to mind when considering the work of the pastor, it is an image which, when we use the word in its ironic sense, has a richness and relevance that are hard to surpass. The folly Paul has in mind is not intrinsic to the pastor's personality – it is not an excuse for being a silly, irresponsible human being – but it is integral to the pastor's role. There are elements of the image which pastors should seek to model themselves on. Care must be taken to imitate those limited aspects of the fool which are wholesome and constructive, and to avoid adopting the role in an undiscriminating way by being mindless idiots. But, more than most other images we are considering,[1] this is one which speaks of the world's opinion of us.

The fool in literature and art

The figure of the fool is well known in the world of literature and art. Take Shakespeare's *King Lear* as an example. King Lear desires to lay down the burdens of office and divide his kingdom between his three daughters. But how is the division to be made? He decides to allocate his kingdom on the basis of how much his daughters can verbalize their love for him. It is a foolish strategy, encouraged by sycophantic courtiers, which succeeds only in ripping Lear's family apart. Mistaking Cordelia's silence for ingratitude, and failing to understand that her love is richer than her tongue, he disowns her and divides his kingdom equally between Goneril and Regan. The play lurches from rage to folly and from folly to tragedy.

In addition to Cordelia, who shows great dignity, one character comes out of the play well, and that is the Fool. He is the court jester who, because of his role, is able to speak truthfully to the king when no-one else would dare. He gets away with it under the guise that no-one takes him seriously. He dares to defy, correct, challenge and instruct. He unmasks the pretensions of kings and courtiers and reveals them as the real fools. In fact, he goes so far as all but to tell Lear that he is a greater fool than he himself is. Lear demands, 'Dost thou call me a fool, boy?' The Fool responds, 'All thy other titles thou has given away; that thou wast born with.'[2] His quick repartee hides a genuine and profound wisdom. But to be a Fool costs. He complains, with good reason, that it is his constant lot to be abused. When threatened with a beating once again, the Fool protests:

> I marvel what kin thou and thy daughters are: they'll have me whipped for speaking true, thou'lt have me whipped for lying; and sometimes I am whipped for holding my peace. I had rather be any kind o' thing than a fool; and yet I would not be thee, nuncle [King Lear]; thou hast pared thy wit o' both sides and left nothing i' the middle ...3

Understandably, John Chrysostom described the fool as 'he who gets slapped'.

The fool, like the little boy who declared that the Emperor had no clothes, is the one who voices the self-evident truth and plain wisdom which others choose to disregard. Os Guinness sums it up well:

> Table-turning is the forte of the ... fool.4 This is the person who appears a fool but is actually the fool-maker, the one who in being ridiculous reveals. The ... fool is the jester; building up expectations in one direction, he shatters them with his punchline, reversing the original meaning and revealing an entirely different one. Masquerading perhaps as the comic butt, he turns the tables on the tyranny of names and labels and strikes subversively for freedom and truth.5

A second illustration of the character of the fool is found in Dostoyevsky's *The Idiot*. The central figure is Prince Leo Nikolayevich Myshkin, whom Dostoyevsky set out to portray as 'a Russian Christ figure who was a holy fool'.6 The portrait he paints is of a man who is naturally humble, who delights to spend his time in the company of servants rather than with those with status, who steps in to absorb the pain of others and who is always an outsider.

Two cameos reveal something of the character of the fool. Prince Myshkin is lodging in the house of Ganya when Nastasya Filippovna calls to announce her decision about the proposal of marriage she has received from Ganya. She has not met Myshkin before and mistakes him for the servant, treating him with contempt. She calls him an idiot and is taken aback when Myshkin apparently knows exactly who she is. But her surprise is nothing in comparison with the consternation she feels shortly afterwards when she discovers that the person at whom she almost swore is, in reality, a prince.

Then, with penetrating insight, there is the comment of Ganya to Prince Myshkin: '… what made me think this morning that you were an Idiot? You notice things other people never notice. One could have a real talk to you, though perhaps one had better not.'[7] Again, we see, that a key characteristic is the apparent deceptiveness of the role. Truth and wisdom are disguised by the apparel and aura of the fool.

Literature constantly plays on the theme of the fool.[8] A related role in the world of the popular arts is that of the circus clown. Clowns give every appearance of being idiots whereas, in fact, they are consummate professionals. They trip and fall about, they put themselves down, they misunderstand and get in the way, they allow themselves to be outwitted, they perform the ridiculous and cause people to laugh at them, but they do it all with perfect timing and flawless artistry. Appearing to be an amateur among professional performers, the clown is, in fact, the supreme professional. The circus clown ranges from the buffoon to the delicate mime artist. Both paint the face and hide their real selves as a means to expressing their personalities with greater liberty.

Charlie Chaplin epitomized the English clown, but the art has largely fallen into disuse in Britain today. It is different in Russia where, according to a newspaper article,[9] the art still alive, well and supremely respected. Its author, Mick Brown, reported that Anatoly Marchevsky was 'a very good clown'. As the principal clown of the Moscow State Circus, he was as respected and decorated as a cosmonaut, a Nobel Prize-winning scientist or a celebrated composer. Clowns are so significant that they not only perform their own individual acts but are the Masters of Ceremonies and take charge of the whole event. Mick Brown thought that what the political leaders needed was to attend the circus more, 'for surely what Russia needs now is cleverness, intelligence and kindness, a sense of the possible and of the ridiculous'. Marchevsky agreed. 'If we had clowns in government life would be much better.' Perhaps there lies true wisdom!

Alastair Campbell has summed up the role of the jester and the clown like this:

> He appears as the essential counterpoise to human arrogance, pomposity and despotism. His unruly behaviour questions the limits of order; his 'crazy' outspoken talk probes the meaning of 'common sense', his unconventional appearance exposes the pride and vanity of those around him; his foolhardy loyalty to 'lost' causes undercuts prudence and self-interest.[10]

In what sense do these wider references to the ironic clown help us to understand the work of the pastor and, in particular, the way in which Paul writes of the image in letters to the Corinthians? They do so by highlighting three themes which are inherent in the image: the fool stands for simplicity, outsidership and weakness.

The fool's simplicity

Fools have a capacity for simplifying the most complicated of issues. Often, in doing so, they miss the point. Their inability to reason well, their lack of awareness of the complexities of issues or of life, can lead them into serious trouble and be a pain to others who see things more deeply. Fools delight in black and white, which is intensely annoying to those who believe in shades of grey.

Yet the fool's mastery of simplicity is as much an asset as a liability. It often gives the ability to go straight to the issue. It enables the fool to penetrate the layers of sophisticated irrelevance, or worse still the layers of delusions and lies, with which the more cultured cloak issues. It leads to a 'refreshing directness' in communication and relationships with others. You certainly know where you stand. The fool is the little boy who, against the wisdom of his day, has the innocence to say, 'The emperor has no clothes.' And it was the little boy, not the crowds, who spoke the truth.

Fools are not overawed by the power or the position of others. It was this kind of foolishness that Jesus taught in the Sermon on the Mount. The 'common-sense' understanding of the world knows that the strong, wealthy, self-sufficient, powerful and arrogant rule the world. To get your own back and get even; to hate your enemies; not to give more than you are asked for; to satisfy your own desires and not let anyone stand in the way of your own ambitions, is the 'common-sense' approach to life. But Jesus turns it on its head. With masterly simplicity he exposes the common-sense way for what it is – 'true folly' that leads only to destruction. By contrast, the way we resist, the way of poverty of spirit, meekness, mercy, non-retaliation, purity and other-directedness, is the genuinely wise and constructive way to live. It is no surprise when Jesus comments that the decision to accept such teaching and come under the authority of his reign requires that we lay aside our adult sophistication and become children (Matt. 18:2–4).

To Paul, the message of the cross is foolishness in the face of 'the wisdom of the world' (1 Cor. 1:18–25). Who in the ancient world could have found it plausible that through the crucifixion of Jesus God was going to save them? Jews certainly wouldn't. Their upbringing schooled them into thinking that whoever hung on a tree was cursed by God (Deut. 21:23). They were looking for a powerful sign from God that he was stepping into the world to save them. They looked for a sign akin to the SAS swinging into action to release the hostages from the Iranian Embassy in London in 1980. A cross was definitely the wrong kind of sign. Nor would Gentiles be convinced of it. To Romans 'the unlucky tree' was reserved for slaves and the insignificant classes. It was an embarrassment, not spoken of directly in polite company. To Greeks, the salvation of the world was expected to come through enlightened philosophy, not through a man dying shamefully on a cross. Gordon Fee rightly concludes, 'No mere human, in his right mind or otherwise, would have dreamed up God's scheme of redemption – through a crucified messiah. It is too preposterous, too humiliating for a God.'[11] And, as Morna Hooker rightly adds, 'Our problem is simply that we are too used to the Christian story; it is difficult for us to grasp the absurdity – indeed, the sheer madness – of the gospel about a crucified saviour which was proclaimed by the first Christians in a world where the cross was the most barbaric form of punishment which men could devise.'[12]

And yet, standing in flat contradiction to the wisdom of the world, the foolishness of Christ's cross revealed God's true wisdom, and its weakness revealed God's true power. As pastors, our message remains the simple and foolish message of the cross. We have no other message to offer the world, and if we try to attract the world by offering something more sophisticated or appealing we will be way off target. Ours is a message of simple folly.

That does not mean that any of us has an excuse for laziness, carelessness or anti-intellectualism, as though we need only parrot a simple formula of salvation. Far from it. To communicate this foolish message requires skill, just as with the deceptively simple antics of the circus clown. Failure to work at how we communicate the message is to indulge in the wrong kind of folly – the folly condemned by Proverbs (see, for example, 16:21–22). Peter Cotterell, my predecessor as Principal of London Bible College, was well known for saying, 'To communicate simply you must understand profoundly.' And he was right. It is this sense that we should constantly pray William Temple's prayer, 'God, who made me simple, make me simpler yet.'[13]

We cannot expect, of course, that such a foolish message will be widely welcomed. It takes courage to speak as a fool in a world which prizes its own misguided wisdom. Yet speak we must. It is here that we must start being fools.

The fool's outsidership

The fool never quite belongs. The court jester performs uncomfortably and is never quite sure what reception he will receive. He is never sure that he is one of the 'in' crowd. Similarly, the attitude to the clown in the circus is ambiguous. The audience recognizes the professionalism of the trapeze artist immediately. The skill of many of the other acts causes wonder and admiration. But the clown is not immediately recognized as one of the professionals. He's not quite at home among the other acts. His role is to be the outsider, to be laughed at.

Alastair Campbell[14] draws attention to the work of Heije Faber on *Pastoral Care in the Modern Hospital.* Faber points out that the clown faces three tensions: 'he is one of many circus acts, yet he has a certain uniqueness, setting him apart from others; he appears and feels like an amateur among highly skilled professionals; and his act

is one of creative spontaneity, yet it demands study and training.'
Faber then has little difficulty in showing how the work of the
chaplain in the modern hospital demonstrates the same
characteristics.

What is true of the chaplain in the hospital is equally true of the
pastoral ministry in general. What is it the pastor does that lay folk
could not do? Different traditions answer that question in different
ways. But for many, especially those affected by the climatic changes
caused by the onset of the charismatic movement and the
rediscovery of 'body ministry' or 'every-member ministry', with its
reaction against 'one-man ministry', there is little if anything left
which others do not and cannot do. All now share in visiting,
caring, counselling, leading worship, praying, preaching and
celebrating communion. And yet, when folk do participate in such
ways, many soon discover that it's harder than they imagined and
that there is still a place for the pastor as such; one who is called,
trained and equipped and who brings a harmony and coherence to
the leadership of the body of Christ.

The pastoral role has increasingly been reduced in size and value.
Historically, all sorts of tasks which once belonged to pastors have
been removed from them.[15] Pastors are no longer called to serve as
doctors, lawyers, schoolteachers or even, nowadays, as counsellors
and social workers. Others, professionals trained in caring and
counselling, are now accorded much higher status in our society and
granted the legal duty to undertake roles which would once have
been part and parcel of the church's pastoral role. Given the
complexity of social-work theory and the intricacy of the competing
psychological approaches to therapy, the pastor does look like a poor
relation – an amateur among professionals.

Many have reacted to this threatening situation by seeking to
equip themselves with knowledge and training which have greater
currency today than theology does. Some, for example, have become
trained counsellors or erected a Christian counselling superstructure
to rival that offered by secular schools. Still others have become
specialists in an area of social work or community need. While not
doubting the sincerity of the motives of those who have done this,
or the value of the path taken, Bryan Wilson is surely right in
suggesting that many have done it as a way of lessening the dis-ease

experienced by the diminishing role and status of the pastor.[16]

Such a reaction needs, however, to be examined carefully. Thomas Oden is among those who have sounded an alarm concerning this trend.[17] He asks what has happened to our classical understanding of pastoral care. Why is it that our textbooks on counselling are full of references to Freud, Jung, Rogers and later psychologists or psychiatrists, but no longer even mention the names of Augustine, Chrysostom, Gregory, Luther, Calvin, Baxter, Wesley or any of the other great pastors of our Christian tradition? Do we no longer place any trust in the wisdom of our own heritage? Furthermore, traditional pastoral methods of spiritual discipline, prayer, Bible guidance, moral choice, meditation, restitution and fasting are being displaced by the use of secularized techniques and cost-benefit analyses of problems.

Is this one of the places where the pastor should be content to remain a fool, an outsider, for the sake of Christ? Does the pastor not have a distinctive contribution to make which, even if despised by the contemporary world, still goes to the heart of the matter because, in the context of ministering to the whole person, it deals particularly with the spiritual and moral aspects of life? Such an approach may mean that we are looked down upon because our credentials do not match the demands of contemporary society and we may well feel uncomfortable as a result. But is that not to adopt the role of the fool? Is it any more than Paul was made to feel by the arrogant and worldly-wise Corinthians, who boasted of their wisdom, wealth and strength in comparison with his folly, poverty and weakness? Indeed, such was the tempestuous relationship between them that Paul went beyond describing himself as a fool and expressed his role more alarmingly as that of 'the scum of the earth, the refuse of the world' (1 Cor. 4:13).[18] To what extent, I wonder, does the contemporary job-description approach to a professionalized ministry make room for the model of the fool as a valid model of ministry?

The roots of the image lay, as Campbell has pointed out,[19] in the Old Testament. The call of the prophets was a call to be fools for God and outsiders in their societies. They were outsiders by definition. Their simple message, usually rejected by the cultured but disintegrating societies they addressed, made them fools. Others thought that society's ills needed more sophisticated answers (usually of a political, economic or libertarian kind) than anything a prophet would ever offer. Some among the prophets were called to be fools in a particular way. They were called to act in bizarre ways in order to convey their message forcefully. So Isaiah was called to parade naked through the streets; Jeremiah to buy a field, hide a waste cloth and carry a yoke; Hosea was called to marry an adulterous wife. Fools indeed! Such behaviour would never make them insiders.

This insight encourages us to give attention to the prophetic nature of pastoral ministry and to challenge the godless and idolatrous way in which society is hurtling towards judgment and the 'Day of the Lord'. If we fulfil such a ministry, then it is guaranteed that we shall be treated as strangers in the world.

The fool's weakness

The heart of Paul's understanding of what it means to be a fool, as the heart of his understanding of what ministry means, is revealed most in 2 Corinthians 10 – 12. Here, foolishness is connected with weakness.

Paul's relationship with his errant child, the church at Corinth, far from improving as a result of any previous correspondence or visits (either by Paul or by intermediaries), has now degenerated further. The problem has been greatly aggravated by the arrival in Corinth of 'super-apostles' (11:5) or false apostles (11:13). Although their identity is subject to debate,[20] the broad outline of their position is clear. They are calling into question Paul's credentials as an apostle. They publish a long agenda of issues where they think he does not measure up. If we can presume that the early chapters of 2 Corinthians mirror their accusations as well as the latter chapters, they are undermining Paul's role as the founder of the church at Corinth by accusing him of vacillation (1:15–17, 23; 2:1); speaking with a forked tongue (1:12); lacking the right commendations (3:1); being untrustworthy with money (8:20–21); behaving in a worldly fashion (10:2); being proud (10:8); not being one of the Twelve (11:5); lacking dignity (11:7) and being deceitful (12:16). By undermining his ministry, they seek, of course, to establish their own.

As if this were not enough to destroy Paul inwardly, from his reply we can hear echoes of other accusations they had mounted. The basic charge seems to have been that Paul was simply not effective enough as a servant of Christ and apostle in the church. He was not a success. There were not enough miracles being performed, not enough converts being won and not enough maturity being achieved to justify Paul's claim to apostleship.

Every pastor knows the experience of being criticized, especially by Christians who think that not enough is being done to change the church in their chosen direction, at least as fast as they would want. Many a pastor, myself included, has been publicly criticized for misleading the church or being a stumbling block in the way of progress. Learning to handle it is crucial to the pastor's ability to continue in ministry. Many have been destroyed and knocked out of ministry by less criticism than Paul received. How did he respond to the avalanche of cynical opposition that threatened to engulf him? The answer: he responded as a fool.

Paul opens this section of the letter by begging the Corinthians to 'put up with a little of my foolishness' (11:1). He openly confesses to speaking as a fool in his own defence (11:21), and concludes with the protest, 'I have made a fool of myself, but you drove me to it' (12:11). In between he defines what he means by foolishness. It is his self-confident boasting (11:16–17). These chapters are full of boasting. But what is it that Paul boasts about? Ironically, he boasts of the things which make him look weak and even more of a failure in the eyes of the super-apostles. Surely he is just playing into their hands! They will trump his reply with a triumphant, 'We told you so.'

Well, not quite. What Paul is doing is to 'answer fools according to their folly, or they will be wise in their own eyes' (Prov. 26:5). He sets out to put the record straight about his achievements, but, in doing so, he turns the whole debate on its head. Paul does not seek to parallel his opponents, but to parody them. He does not seek to outdo them, but to undermine them. He boasts about the very things one would normally wish to hide. He glories in matters which are shameful and spotlights matters that magnify weakness. He answers them ironically. He does so by adopting a part; by putting on a clown's make-up and hiding his real self.

James Denney's classic commentary on 2 Corinthians puts it like this:

> He adopts the policy of his adversaries and proceeds to enlarge on his services to the church; but with magnificent irony, he first assumes the mask of a fool. It is not the genuine Paul who figures here; it is Paul playing a part to which he has been compelled against his will acting in a character as remote as possible from his own.[21]

Since Denney's day, research has thrown Paul's approach into even sharper relief. Paul is responding not simply by parodying the approach of the false apostles, but by using a range of rejoinders which were customary among Hellenistic public speakers of his day – among them, comparison, self-praise and irony.[22] Each was employed according to certain rhetorical conventions. Cicero, for example, argued that, for any orator in a dispute, there were 'four ways to cultivate good will: by references to (a) ourselves, (b) our opponents, (c) what we might call the jury, and (d) the case of the situation itself'.[23] Similarly, Plutarch had written 'On Praising Oneself Inoffensively', in which he argued that there were circumstances in which self-praise, normally considered unworthy, was permitted. Self-glorification was admissible if it served a good end and did the hearers good, and when others failed to offer the praise they should (see 12:11).[24]

Doubtless Paul has suffered from his opponents using the conventions of his time. He now turns the tables on them and uses the same conventions, although not slavishly, to his own ends. He employs them to magnificent effect in the defence of true apostolic ministry. Note how he does it. Paul and the super-apostles have much in common (11:22), but they, judging from the 'echoes', boast of personal boldness (10:1–11), missionary achievements (10:12–16), eloquent speech (11:5–6), financial support (11:7–12), ecstatic experiences (5:12–13; 12:1–4) and miraculous accomplishments (12:11–12), all of which have eluded Paul. By contrast, Paul boasts of all the things that make him appear weak, and so things which cast him back on to God. He boasts of physical hardships (11:23–27), psychological pressure (11:28–29), personal indignity (11:30–33), one dated spiritual experience (12:1–6) and a painful handicap (12:7–10). The portrait drawn reveals him to have been anything but a continuous success in ministry.

The details are interesting. The catalogue of hardships is written with striking detail. He counts the number of times he's been lashed, beaten with rods, stoned and shipwrecked. These are vivid memories that have not disappeared as the bruises have faded. He senses the loneliness and isolation of leadership intensely. While he whips through the list of hardships, he stumbles over one memory. He escaped from Damascus in a basket lowered out of a window outside the city wall. Why does he mention this incident in such detail? Calvin said it was because it was his 'first apprenticeship in persecution' – a raw recruit in training.[25] But it is likely to be more than that. Furnish[26] relates it to the *corona muralis*, the 'wall crown' which was awarded to the first soldier to go over the wall into an enemy city. The crown was a high military honour and fashioned in the shape of a turret in gold. Paul, by contrast, is boasting that his *corona muralis* is being awarded for being first over the wall out of, not into, a hostile city. It must have gone against all Paul's pioneering instincts to flee. But he did, and that now has become the credential about which he boasts.

Similarly, his record of spiritual experience is, in truth, nothing to boast about. Far from having regular and intimate encounters with God, he can drag up only one such experience fourteen years previously, which he is quite incapable of saying anything about. And he can speak about this at all only because he distances himself from it and purports that it happened to a third person. This is a far cry from the boasting of his opponents who appear to have a constant hotline open to heaven. And, whatever the thorn in the flesh might have been (2 Cor. 12:7), we know that it was real, painful, recurring and humiliating. Although it was 'a messenger of Satan', God used it to demonstrate that his grace is experienced personally and conveyed to others by embracing weakness, not by avoiding it. All this is so that God, and God alone, might have the glory (1 Cor. 1:31).

To what extent does Paul's approach provide a model for today's pastor? Few can boast (although some can) of the catalogue of hardships which Paul experienced. If that is so, is it not equally dangerous to seek to answer one's critics in the manner adopted by Paul? Is not Paul in a league of his own and consequently unable to serve as a model for us today, as some have argued?[27] But surely there are some things we can learn.

Being a fool brings great relief to those who struggle with the 'superstars' who inhabit the church today, and with the secular superstars who are held up to pastors as a model. In vivid contrast to their success, we can gladly don the mask of the fool, knowing that the fool experiences more of, and ministers more in, the real grace of God than those who appear successful on the surface (10:7). This image will save us from falling into the temptation to talk about ourselves instead of our Lord. There are some popular preachers who are full of stories about their travels, their converts, even their miracles. When they have finished preaching, we know a lot about them but very little about the gospel. Such preaching is in profound conflict with our calling as servants of Jesus, and particularly in conflict with the portrait of being a fool for Christ.

Criticism will always be a fact of pastoral life. Rarely is it right to meet it head on, although occasionally it might be necessary. More frequently, we fallible pastors have something to learn from our critics. They may just be right. But if not, and if the criticism is unjust, we must avoid playing the game of one-upmanship; boasting about ourselves and imposing our own authority to crush our opponents. Rather, we must try to adopt strategies which will get behind the animosity and resentment that so easily grow in the soil of criticism. As with Christ, there are times to suffer in silence. With the sage, there are times when a 'soft answer turns away wrath'. Like Paul, we may seek to undermine our critics by exposing their folly for what it is and by laughing at ourselves. Our aim, like his, must be to cause people to look more deeply at the meaning of the gospel itself and at the spiritual implications of the criticisms they unjustly mount.

The heart of the matter for Paul is that his God revealed himself most when Christ 'was crucified in weakness' (13:4). Weakness is not a matter of shame, but both a fact of life and a divine strategy. It is not to be accepted with mere resignation, nor do we need to summon up strength to 'grin and bear it', or to find the resources to cope within ourselves. Instead, weakness is the field in which God's grace operates. It is, then, an essential characteristic of Christian living and, even more, of Christian ministry. So when the ups and downs of Christian ministry take place, we are moulded and shaped into the likeness of Christ. We are called to be fools and to identify with his cross and his resurrection.

Conclusion

Jim Wallis concluded his book *The Call to Conversion*[28] with this cry: 'May God call us to such foolishness.' May we, indeed, accept the role of the fool, in order that we might preach with simplicity the foolish message of the cross; live as outsiders in, and irritants to, a dying world; and nurture and care from a position of weakness, knowing that it is only when we are in that position that God's grace can flow through us and that God's glory will be unblemished.

Questions for reflection

1. To what extent am I prepared to be a 'fool for Christ'?

2. Am I content to preach the simple message of 'Christ crucified', or have I allowed my preaching to move away from the simplicity of the gospel?

3. Have I ever honestly confronted how intimidated I feel as a Christian pastor called to serve in a world of sophisticated professionals? Is such folly integral to my calling?

4. In what ways, if any, do I feel myself to be exercising ministry as 'an outsider'?

5. If I were to rebut my critics along the lines of Paul's approach in 2 Corinthians 10 – 13, what would compose my catalogue of foolish boasts?

6. How do I handle my critics? Does Paul give any help towards finding a better approach?

7. What is my 'thorn in the flesh'? Have I learned to hear God say, 'My grace is sufficient for you, for my power is made perfect in weakness' (2 Cor. 12:9)?

5

Parent

'... like a mother ... as
a father ...' (1 Thess. 2:7, 11).

Bible translations can sometimes prove very inconvenient for preachers. Many a preacher has fallen foul of a new translation. A favourite sermon has been constructed on the basis of the English wording of the AV or RSV.[1] But then the congregation moves on to use the Good News Bible or the NIV, and the structure of the sermon no longer makes sense because the vocabulary has been changed. It's a salutary reminder to all preachers to dig beneath any translation and discover the original meaning of the words and the original form in which they were written.

I encountered such an inconvenience as I came to prepare the next image, that of the pastor in the New Testament. This was going to be a chapter on the phrase 'gentle as a nurse' (1 Thess. 2:7). The image of the nurse as one who tenderly cares for her children is found in the AV and the NRSV. Unfortunately, it was not to be found in the NIV, the version I use. Why not?

The reason is that the word translated 'nurse' by some is the Greek word *trophos*. It could legitimately be translated 'nurse'. But it might equally be translated 'mother', and in the context 'mother' seems to be the more appropriate translation for two reasons. First,

Paul describes the *trophos* as caring for her own children or her little children. The picture, then, is not of a professional nurse caring for someone else's older children, but of a mother wet-nursing her own offspring. Secondly, in the wider context of 1 Thessalonians 2, Paul seems to balance the feminine image of his work, 'like a mother' (v. 7), with the masculine image of his work, 'as a father' (v. 11). We grasp Paul's description of his work better, therefore, if we see the image as one of parenthood – female and male – rather than limiting it to that of the nurse which, at least as far as contemporary society goes, might lead to some wrong conclusions about ministry. Nursing has become a highly skilled and professional occupation. Nurses deal with patients with some degree of objectivity. Such an image would lead us in the wrong direction if we are seeking to understand what Paul is saying.

The gentle nurse

Having said that, we ought not to dismiss the image of the nurse, since Paul is thinking in terms of a mother *nursing* her children. Phrases referring to the gentleness of a nurse were common parlance in the ancient world, especially among philosophers. Paul seems to be tapping into a broader secular theme in what he writes. An understanding of that theme helps us to unlock his burden about pastoral ministry.

The ancient world had many itinerant public speakers or philosophers who sought to gain a hearing. Many of them were hucksters who had no credentials and even less substance. Frequent allegations were made against them for a whole host of reasons. Common complaints accused them of being greedy and in error, of flattering their followers and of haranguing their audiences and treating them harshly.

In the eyes of some, the apostle Paul was little different from these wandering philosophers. The accusations he faces bear a striking similarity to those mounted against other public speakers. He is accused of being a failure (1 Thess. 2:1–2); of teaching error (v. 3); of deceiving his hearers (v. 3); of pleasing people by flattery (vv. 4–5) and of being in it for financial gain (v. 5). Neither his motives nor his character, it was being said, would stand up to close examination. His sudden departure from Thessalonica, together with the apparent failure of some of his teaching (as, for example, his teaching about the second coming which still had not occurred although some in the fellowship had already died), meant that he had to defend himself and say why he was not a charlatan and why his teaching should be taken seriously.

There are clear echoes of such allegations in the writings of Dio Chrysostom, the orator who became a Cynic philosopher and who was one of Paul's younger contemporaries. Given that the world of wandering philosophers was one of accusation and counter-accusation, we are aware not only of the allegations made but also of how they rebutted them. Paul's response to the accusations against him shows an awareness of this wider discussion among phil-osophers, and especially of the debate about whether it was most helpful to treat one's hearers with severity or gentleness. Different types of philosophers operated in different ways. According to Malherbe,[2] Dio Chrysostom identifies four ways of operating.

First, there were *resident philosophers* who 'do not appear in public at all, and prefer not to run the risk, possibly because they despair of being able to improve the masses'. They served as 'chaplains' to households or at court. Their uppermost concern was their own dignity. Chrysostom characterizes them as 'make-believe athletes who refuse to enter the stadium where they would enter the contest of life'.

Second, there were the *hucksters*. These ignoble people had no knowledge to impart to others but, since they had to make a living, it did not stop them from standing on street corners, in alley-ways and at temple gates, shouting and, of course, then passing around the hat. They served no useful purpose but were out for their own glory, pleasure and money. Essentially, they deceived people.

Third were the *rhetoricians*. They tended to have no real involvement with the events at which they spoke. There was often little substance to what they said, and their teaching resulted in nothing positive. Often they, too, were in it for their own ends and not to benefit their listeners. They were like physicians who, instead of curing their patients, amused them.

Fourth, there were the *confident types*. They believed that the philosopher should speak with boldness, outspokenness and frankness. Not only would this boldness benefit the hearers, but it would give the philosopher an independence and freedom which befitted the profession itself. They treated the masses with a certain amount of disdain, and felt that among the variety of weapons to be used were abuse, scorn and harshness. Only words which were caustic and severe would serve to deliver people from their unenlightened lives and situations. Nothing less than surgery, cautery and strong drugs, according to Pseudo-Diogenes, would cure the disease from which the masses suffered. Flattery and gentleness simply betrayed ignorance of the hearers' true condition. These philosophers delighted to dwell on the shortcomings of their audiences, since they had a very pessimistic view of human nature. But such philosophers also frequently had to make a hurried exit before the mob got out of hand!

In this context 'it became customary to contrast the harshness of a certain kind of *parrēsia* (boldness, outspokenness) with gentle speech such as that of a nurse who knows her charge'.[3] At the time, nurses were apparently considered with great affection by many. They were the ones who had cared for men in their tender years and had never been irritable, disagreeable or hot-tempered.[4]

In this debate, the apostle Paul definitely comes down on the side of the nurses. Malherbe points out that it is striking that Paul does not balance the image of gentleness with any reference to scolding or abusiveness. 'Paul's demeanour was characteristically gentle.'[5]

If, elsewhere (see 1 Cor. 4:14 – 5:5), there was a place for plain speaking, then Paul believed, with Plutarch, that it was medicine which must be applied with care and only in the right circumstances.[6] For the most part, people needed to be treated with gentleness, especially in situations where they were struggling. Plutarch's view was that the difficult circumstances 'in which the unfortunate find themselves leave no room for frank speaking and sententious saws, but they do require gentle usage and help. When children fall down, the nurses do not rush up and berate them, but they take them up, wash them, and straighten their clothes, and, after all this is done, they then rebuke and punish them.'[7]

All this may well have lain behind Paul's allusion to himself as 'gentle as a nurse' or as 'caring like a mother'. He states quite clearly that the manner and style of the true Christian pastor must be gentle. In advocating such a position, Paul stands in stark contrast not only to many of the itinerant field preachers of his day but also to many pastors and preachers of our own. Many have more of the style of the 'confident ones' than of the 'gentle nurse'. With a pessimistic view of their congregation, let alone of those outside, they believe the only way to dispel their spiritual dullness and penetrate their hardness is to be outspoken. What motivates it, in truth, is often an authoritarian personality or a lack of true experience of grace.

Some masochistic congregations have either grown so used to being whipped by their pastors and preachers, or are so deluded into thinking that it is a necessary spiritual method, that they come to love it. Many believers are never so happy as when they are being 'challenged'. Whether the multitude of 'challenges' they have faced during the course of their careers as disciples has made any practical difference is questionable.

The temptation is not confined, however, to a few. Every pastor is outspoken at times. Even the most gentle among us occasionally cherish some pet project so much more than our congregations do that we find ourselves whipping the reluctant into line or berating them for lethargy. Tiredness can easily lead to discouragement. When it does, we often take it out on the congregation and begin to preach irritably or with a pained touchiness. In these circumstances we should probably take practical steps to stand back and disengage a little from our work. We are probably over-involved. Regardless of whether we take such practical action to gain a truer perspective of our people or not, we ought always to seek to model ourselves on this image and, like Paul, appeal to people 'by the meekness and gentleness of Christ' (2 Cor. 10:1).

The tender mother

With that background in mind we can now turn to look more fully at what Paul says about the image of a mother 'caring for her little children'.[8] The picture is one of provision and nourishment. It derives from the early days of a child's life when the mother provides milk from her own breast for the child. It is that crucial period when the child learns (or, sadly, fails to learn) bonding, attachment and security. In developing this image, Paul draws attention to three aspects of it.

Affection

It is a cosy picture, and why not? Paul's best defence against the accusations he faced from the Thessalonians is to protest, 'We loved you so much ...' (v. 8). Howard Marshall comments, 'The element of tender loving care for the children is expressed sufficiently [in these verses to] convey the idea of taking them in one's arms, fondling them and keeping them warm and safe ... just as a mother-bird broods over her young.'[9]

Most mothers do care and feel for their children in this way. They worry about their well-being, strive to provide their needs even at their own expense, and always seek the best for their children. They refuse to be put off loving their child in spite of the nights interrupted by their crying baby, which leave them exhausted the next day. Nor are they disconcerted when the child is sick at embarrassing moments. Nor will they allow the terrible twos, or the traumatic threes, or even the frightful fours, to erode the relationship of love which is instinctive in every mother.

Perhaps, then, the most basic question any pastor faces is whether we love our congregation or not. Without a relationship of love, the raw material out of which pastoral ministry can be created is missing. Naturally, there will be times of exasperation, the need on occasions for admonition, periods of disappointment, and even some degree of alienation. But when those times occur, there is even more the need for love. Love helps one triumph over exasperation and continue to exercise patience. We know that discipline and admonition are effective only if given within a loving relationship. Without that it is likely to be ineffective, if not downright harmful. Love can go on hoping even through disappointment. And love will go on reaching out during periods of alienation or rejection.

For all the shortcomings of the church which we who are in the thick of it feel most intensely, Philip Hacking is surely right when he says:

I would also bear testimony that it is the local church where I am most known and where I can be most hurt that I can experience that richness at the deepest level. It is comparatively easy to enjoy fellowship in a fortnight's ministry in some overseas church. It is another thing to be real in the rough and tumble of life, where the warts are very evident on our faces and the faces of our fellow Christians. Yet there love can dominate and the church can be the greatest audio-visual presentation of all time.[10]

True affection masters all shortcomings. It builds strong relational bonds and so provides a climate in which healthy growth and development can take place in an environment of security. A little more affection and a little less admonition may go a long way in helping many of our churches to grow.

Self-giving

It would be virtually impossible to list what a mother gives to her child, although some have tried. One could begin to list the meals cooked, the washing done, the tidying-up undertaken, the hours spent listening, the petrol used up in ferrying to and fro, the messes cleared up, the wounds healed and so on. But we know that listing the jobs is not the point. It is not so much that a mother gives time, money, food and support, as that she gives herself. Home is the one place where the limits of the job description don't apply and where the boundaries of time or task that mark other relationships don't count.

This is the point Paul makes about his relationship to the Thessalonians. It was not, he argued, that he came among them as a professional philosopher in order to dispense a new teaching to them and then withdraw. That would have been far too superficial and cold. His delight lay in sharing with them 'not only the gospel of God but our lives as well, because you had become so dear to us' (v. 8). In this particular instance it meant that Paul supported himself, working all hours to do so, in order that he might preach the gospel without receiving any financial support from them. This was no easy option. It meant toil and hardship as far as he was concerned. But no matter, it was in the nature of the relationship that he should give himself without an eye to the hours he was working or the money he was making. The point was, like any good mother, he was giving *himself*, not just his services, to the Thessalonians. Self-giving is what mothers do.

Patterns of ministry have changed in recent years. Many, myself included, have benefited from working from a church-based office rather than from home. For good reasons, there has been a greater awareness of the need to be more protective towards family life and to guard time off and time with one's spouse. Greater attention has been given, perhaps rightly, to more thoughtful terms and conditions of employment. But, through all this, we must never lose sight of the fact that the essence of the ministry is seen in the kind of tender relationship one sees between a mother and a child. And it is impossible to limit that. Its ideal, to which we must strive, is seen in self-giving.

John Calvin sums it up:

> A mother in nursing her child makes no show of authority and does not stand on her dignity ... A mother in rearing her children reveals a wonderful and extraordinary love, because she spares no trouble or effort, avoids no care, is not wearied by their coming and going, and gladly gives her own life blood to be drained.[11]

Home is not a hotel. Mothers are not servants. They do not work to contract. The relationship is one of covenant love and self-giving. All that makes the nursing mother, according to Paul, an ideal illustration of pastoral ministry.

Gentleness

The third and most prominent characteristic of the mother to which Paul draws attention here is that of gentleness. We have seen the background to Paul's insistence that his relationship with the Thessalonians should be marked by gentleness. He insists on it again in the very different circumstances of 2 Timothy 2:24–25, where he teaches Timothy how to instruct opponents about the error of their ways.

My guess is that Paul did not find it easy to be gentle. The way he dealt with Peter at Antioch (Gal. 2:11–21) John Mark and Barnabas after Pamphylia (Acts 15:36–41) and the Roman authorities at Philippi (Acts 16:37–40) suggests that gentleness was not a natural quality for Paul. He would probably not have been a go-getting pioneering church-planter had it been an inbred characteristic. It was something which the educative grace of the Holy Spirit had had to school him in. The secret which produced the transformation may well have been the way in which he had reflected on the unlimited patience of God in his own life (1 Tim. 1:16). If God has been so patient with him, with the result that he could become a display case for the gospel, then, surely it was incumbent on him to be patient and gentle with others too.

Some see gentleness as coming dangerously close to compromising one's integrity. To others it smacks of lethargy and a lack of urgency in completing the task. But the more significant thing for all of us who find it difficult to be gentle is surely to realize that it is the way of our crucified Saviour and the path which he calls us still to tread. If we are worried about compromise or lack of achievement, we should reflect that the cross failed on neither count. Rather, the gentle way of Jesus Christ at Calvary was the biggest statement of defiant integrity and the most amazingly transformative action, leading as it did to the resurrection, that the world has ever known.

Paul's use of the image of a mother is not exhausted by his reference to it in 1 Thessalonians 2. A similar thought, developing the idea that a mother nourishes her children with food appropriate to their age, milk first and then meat, occurs in 1 Corinthians 3:1–2. In Galatians 4:19 he develops the image in a different way. There he compares his experience with the Galatian Christians to the painful experience of giving birth to the same child, not once but twice. He's been through the experience of pregnancy and delivery once, at the time of their conversion, but now, given their tendency to forsake truth for heresy, he is going through it all over again 'until Christ is formed in you'. In speaking like this he neatly highlights the agony and the ecstasy of being a pastor.

Honest attention needs to be paid to the feminine character of this image. It stands in sharp contrast to the macho male world of the philosophers yesterday and of leadership today. It rebukes us for the exclusively masculine perspectives we often exalt in discussing pastoral leadership; a rebuke which carries added weight because the image is one that finds its origin in God himself. When Moses faced another difficult patch in leading the children of Israel he complains to God, 'Why do you tell me to carry them in my arms, as a nurse carries an infant?' (Num. 11:12). In giving voice to the burden he felt he shows he has understood the heart of God.

Similarly, Isaiah 49:15–16 voices God's anguish over his people in feminine terms.

> Can a mother forget the baby at her breast
>   and have no compassion on the child she has borne?
> Though she may forget,
>   I will not forget you!
> See, I have engraved you on the palms of my hands;
>   your walls are ever before me.

Hosea expresses God's love for Israel in terms reminiscent of a mother lavishing care upon a growing child, rejoicing in their early steps and always being on hand to cuddle them when the bumps and bruises come (Hos. 11:1–2). I have no doubt that God is appropriately spoken of as our 'father.' But this should not blind us to the maternal pictures of God which are also present within Scripture. In using the gentleness of a nursing mother as an ideal image for pastoral ministry, Paul is not simply underlining the value of gentleness as an effective technique. He is doing much more than that. He is saying that our ministry derives from the ministry of God himself towards his people. To minister as a mother is to minister in God's way.

The model father

At the same time, to minister in God's way is also to minister as a father. The belief was ancient. Moses testified that God carried his people through the desert 'as a father carries his son' (Deut. 1:31). But it was only with the coming of Jesus Christ that any real experience of God as father developed as he taught his disciples to relate to God as *Abba*. Although this reinforces the idea that all our ministry is derived from God's ministry to us, it is probably not this that Paul had in mind when he spoke of himself as dealing 'with each of you as a father deals with his own children' (1 Thess. 2:11). After all, Jesus has instructed his disciples not to call 'anyone on earth "father", for you have one Father, and he is in heaven' (Matt. 23:9). Paul is hardly likely to have gone against such an unambiguous instruction by his Lord (even if many have subsequently done so!). He was not claiming a title, either here or elsewhere, when he describes his ministry as like the relationship of a father to his children; he was simply using a metaphor from contemporary experience.

The Roman father was a powerful person with legal and financial authority over his children extending beyond childhood days and into adulthood. But the power exercised by the father was also balanced by 'a bond of reciprocal, dutiful affection'.[12] We may shy away from the image, since patriarchy has become politically incorrect, but that should not stop us from trying to understand what it would have meant when Paul used it, nor should we ignore the implications it may have for pastoral ministry today.

Paul uses the concept widely in relation to churches he founded[13] (for example, 1 Cor. 4:15), not to boast of his authority over them but to express his paternal love and highlight the deep bond between them. Fathers not only had rights, they had very significant responsibilities towards their children, which included guarding, providing, nurturing and teaching them. It is these aspects of fatherhood which come to the fore in 1 Thessalonians 2. Again, three aspects call for comment.

Individual care

Paul's fatherly role involved dealing with 'each of you' (v. 11). The father is not in the business of mass producing. The father knows that each child is a unique person and has his or her own needs, character, strengths, fears, weaknesses, strengths, potential and personality. Many have been amazed how the same parents can have produced children who, brought up the same way and in the same environment, turn out to be so different from each other. So it is spiritually. What encourages one discourages another. What motivates one drives another into his or her shell. What spurs one to action induces another to laziness.

It is a point which Paul amplifies later in 1 Thessalonians. As he draws his letter to a close, he urges the church to 'warn those who are idle, encourage the timid, help the weak' (5:14). Differing strategies are appropriate to different people. There can be no blanket approach that will get through to all. Not everyone is the same, nor is everyone at the same point on their spiritual journey. Some believers are young and commit sin out of ignorance. Some are mature and informed, and commit sin wilfully. Others are old and tired and have little strength left to resist temptation. The first need instruction, the second rebuke and the third support. To treat them all the same is a failure in pastoral technique and a failure of love. The individual needs to be known if the pastor is to be effective in producing growth towards maturity in Christ.

The early church fathers took this issue very seriously. Gregory the Great in his *Pastoral Rule* outlined thirty-six contrasting types of church member. They included the rich and the poor, the whole and the sick, the slothful and the passionate, the obstinate and the fickle, the troublemakers and the peacemakers, the patient and the impatient, and so on. He described the strengths and weaknesses of every case, and argued that even those types which appear to be the most sound (the whole, the peacemakers, the patient ones, *etc.*) have potential weaknesses which need to be addressed. He then gives careful guidance on how each one was to be pastored appropriately.

Chrysostom stressed the peril of not giving individual pastoral care. The approach must fit the person 'lest, while wishing to mend what is torn, you make the rent worst, and in your zealous endeavours to restore what is fallen, you make the ruin the greater'. Gregory of Nazianzus summed it up like this:

> Some are led by doctrine, others trained by example, some need the spur, others the curb; some are sluggish and hard to rouse to the good, and must be spurred by being smitten with the word; others are immodestly fervent in spirit, with impulses difficult to restrain like thoroughbred colts, who run wide of the turning post, and to improve them the word

must have a restraining and checking influence.[14]

Pastoral ministry, then, is not adequately fulfilled when only conducted wholesale from the pulpit or in any other general way. It demands a fatherly knowledge of every individual and a personal application of God's word to them in ways which are appropriate to them personally.

Teaching

Paul describes the content of this individual care as 'encouraging, comforting and urging you to live lives worthy of God' (v. 12). Here the educative role of the father comes to the fore. Ernest Best rightly claims that 'in the ancient world ... the father bore a special role in relation to the education of his children and it is very difficult to separate the teaching and fatherly roles in Paul. Presumably he himself would never have done so.'[15]

It was the father's responsibility to teach and Paul amply demonstrates that he fulfilled this responsibility with care, enthusiasm and skill. His concern was to enable people to understand their God and his gospel more and more and to grasp the full implications of it all for their daily lives. The pastor who cares but does not teach is guilty of a dereliction of duty. It is not enough just to accept people as they are (although that is always fundamental to a relationship based on grace). It is essential to instruct them further so that they might grow beyond what they currently are, understand 'God's grace in all its truth' (Col. 1:6) and go on to maturity.

Paul addresses the Thessalonians as 'little children'. As yet, they are immature. Appropriately, therefore, his instruction involved a mixed approach of exhortation, emphatic declaration and consolation.[16] In other circumstances his teaching would be a more measured or sustained exposition of the gospel, as in Romans; a joyful exploration of faith, as in Philippians; or the deep reflection of an aged parent, as in the pastoral letters. The style of teaching varied according to the need. But the commitment to teaching never wavered at all.

Nor did Paul ever waver in his insistence that there was truth to be taught which could be distinguished from error, and a right tradition of belief which needed to be passed on and guarded in the face of attempts to alter or dilute it (for example, 2 Tim. 1:13–14). It is this, the apostolic faith, which pastors have a duty to teach. Such teaching requires the involvement of the mind, as well as the heart,[17] and we should never be ashamed of the intellectual content of our faith. It requires pastors to exercise their minds and have an understanding of their faith. Study, therefore, becomes an essential, not an added extra, of pastoral ministry. Moreover, it is not only we pastors who should study and use our minds. It is important to urge those we are encouraging to grow to maturity in Christ to do the same. A Christian faith which is all heart and no head, all experience and no thought, all Spirit and no truth, is condemned to remain an immature faith. Teaching, then, is vital.

Modelling

Modelling was an important part of the educational philosophy of the ancient world in two respects.[18] First, any teacher was expected to serve as a model for his pupils. Learning from the teacher's example was intrinsic to their educational method. Secondly, it was inherent in the father–son relationship. The son would learn from the father by imitating him. A typical example is seen in the advice of Isocrates to Demonicus. 'I have produced a sample of the nature of Hipponicus [your father], after whom you should pattern your life as after an example, regarding his conduct as your law, and striving to imitate and emulate your father's virtue.'[19]

Far from stunting the development of the individual child and cramping his style, which is the fear we might have today, this approach was viewed with favour. The son would, by this means, grow to the full potential of what he was by virtue of his birth. Only by emulating his father would a child attain to the fullest expression of his natural inheritance.

Paul builds on this common assumption in relation to the churches of which he was the founding father (see 1 Cor. 15 – 16; Gal. 4:12; Phil. 3:17; 1 Thess. 1:6), and either invites or commends their imitation of him. They are not called to copy him in everything. He does not, for example, expect all of them to become itinerant missionaries or, however commendable the state was, to remain single. They are to copy him in so far as he copies Christ. His closeness to Christ is the crucial issue. Hence he can say to the Thessalonians that 'you became imitators of us and of the Lord' (1:6). It is essentially a call to discover the wonder of the gospel, to develop Christian character and to duplicate the experience of the cross. In these respects they are to be 'like father, like son'.

Like it or not, pastors still function as models for their congregations today. It is frightening to observe the impact pastors have on their churches. You can tell a lot about a pastor's passion in ministry (whether it be counselling, evangelism, social action, Puritan theology or charismatic experience) from listening to the way his or her members talk. One might even pick up some of the pastor's mannerisms by observing his or her congregation. Pastors are influential models. We cannot pretend otherwise, nor, biblically, should we try to do so.

That being so, it makes us look carefully at what people see in us and then reproduce in their own lives. Perhaps the primary model of Christianity they observe today, whatever its more particular complexion might be, is one of frenetic busyness, as we rush from one meeting to another and exhibit a programme-based activism. Christlikeness of character and closeness to God may not be the thing that comes readily to their minds as the component that they should be imitating. Yet for Paul that was the most pressing item on the agenda of imitation.

Conclusion

What is impressive in the image of the parent is its symmetry. To paraphrase James Denney,[20] the tender fondness of a mother's love is balanced by the educative wisdom of a father. Pastors are called to demonstrate both feminine and masculine characteristics. And an equilibrium is to be sought between them. Neither is to be exercised at the expense of the other. It is in the balance of being gentle, like a mother, and dealing with each one as a father, that children can grow to maturity and reach their full potential in Christ.

Questions for reflection

1. Am I given to flattering my congregation or to outspokenness?

2. To what extent do I love the people God has given me to care for?

3. What is my reaction to being told that the self-giving of a mother is to be a model for my pastoral ministry? If I am honest, do I resist such a demanding relationship? If I welcome it, how do I cope with such a large and demanding family and retain my own sanity?

4. Under what circumstances do I find it difficult to be gentle with the people I pastor? Do I find myself 'driving them' rather than 'leading them'? How can I avoid doing so?

5. Are my pastoral teaching and guidance shaped by the need of the individual, or do I issue blanket assessments, advice and remedies to situations?

6. If I am a model, what is it that people will imitate in me?

7. Am I more prone to act as a mother or as a father? Is there a serious imbalance that needs correcting? If so, what steps can I take to do so?

6
Pilot

'...those with gifts of
navigation' (1 Cor. 12:28).

I was privileged to grow up by the sea, in the little town of
Teignmouth, on the south coast of Devon. To gain entry to the
harbour, situated just in the mouth of the River Teign, is difficult.
Boats have to negotiate their passage through a 160-foot-wide
channel, taking care not to go aground on the immense sandbank
that lies opposite the harbour wall. A pilot is needed to assist with
navigation. It was, therefore, no real surprise to read of 'the mayhem
that happened when the skipper said, "I'll do it my way ..."'[1] A
Russian skipper, Lev Zaytsev, took the pilot on board his 1,560-ton
ship, the *Lagoda 103*, but then ignored his advice. The prosecuting
solicitor told the court in which Zaytsev found himself:

> The first moored boat hit belonged to harbourmaster Reg
> Matthews [our old next door neighbour!]. The *Lagoda* struck
> its pulpit and snapped its moorings. Next it hit a 16-ft seine-
> netter, went straight over the top of it and sunk it. The
> fishing net inside wound itself around the port propeller.
> [It] then hit a motor cruiser called the *Quintessa* and
> another called the *Madge Wildfire* with two people on board.

As the ship continued with Zaytsev operating the controls, the ship slowed right down because of the fouled propeller and was at the mercy of winds and the tide.

One might have guessed the explanation. 'When the police arrived Zaystev was in a very drunken condition.'

Pilots are essential.

The image in wider perspective

The image of the pastor as a pilot, or navigator, is one of the most evocative in Scripture. It occurs only once and then suffers from the misfortune of being translated in a misleading way by most English versions. In 1 Corinthians 12:28, Paul is writing of the gifts which the Holy Spirit gives to the church and refers, in his list, to *kybernēseis*, to those, that is, with gifts of administration, as it is frequently translated. The noun, *kybernētēs*, is used on only two other occasions in the New Testament, and on both occasions in the ordinary sense of a pilot or sea-captain (Acts 27:11; Rev. 18:17). So to imply that the gift of the *kybernētēs* is to do with administration in the modern sense of paper-pushing or organizing events or programmes (vital as those tasks are) is unfortunate. It was, in fact, the word used by the Greeks to speak of the art of government, of guiding the ship of the state. It is, therefore, the gift of helmsmanship, of steersmanship or of navigation. The *kybernētēs* was the person with his hand on the tiller. It parallels the gifts spoken of by Paul in Romans 12:8 when he writes: 'If your gift … is leadership, then govern diligently.'

Unlike the image of the shepherd, 'pilot' is nowhere applied directly to God or to Jesus Christ. It was a concept, however, with which Jesus would have been at home, having grown up as a Galilean and having crossed its storm-prone lake so often. Indeed, at least, one gospel incident seems to present him in this light, as he rescued his distressed disciples and navigated them safely to the other side (Mark 5:35). If, as some scholars have suggested, the original readers of Mark's gospel were second-generation disciples suffering persecution for their faith in the city of Rome, then this incident was particularly poignant. The Christ who had rescued his disciples and commanded the wind and the waves to be quiet was more than capable of piloting his people safely through their experience of persecution.

Alexander Maclaren once referred to Jesus as the 'Pilot of the Galilean lake'. In his exposition of the risen Christ preparing breakfast on the beach for his tired disciples who had fished all night without catching anything (John 21:1–14), Maclaren writes this:

> So here is a vision to cheer us all. Life must be full of toil and of failure. We are on the midnight sea, and have to tug, weary and wet, at a heavy oar, and to haul an often empty net. But we do not labour alone. He comes to us across the storm, and is with us in the night, a most real, because unseen, Presence. If we accept the guidance of His directing word, His indwelling Spirit, and His all-sufficient example, and seek to ascertain His will in outward Providence, we shall not be left to waste our strength in blunders, nor shall our labour be in vain. In the morning light we shall see Him standing serene on the steadfast shore. The 'Pilot of the Galilean lake' will guide our frail boat through the wild surf that marks the breaking of the sea of life on the shore of eternity …[2]

So even if the image is not applied directly in the Bible to Jesus, it is certainly apt. Many of us would benefit from meditating on the picture of Jesus as the pilot of the church we serve, and as the one who is safely, if all unseen, navigating the course of our ministries. To look to him as the pilot-in-chief would take the pressure off us, suffering as we often do from the delusion that our ministries depend for their effectiveness on our energies, gifts, skills and resources alone. And it would help to place the responsibility back where it already rightly belongs, into his capable hands. Knowing that he is *the* pilot is the source of great comfort and reassurance, especially in days when the sea gets stormy.

The early church picked up the image and elaborated it, using it frequently both to describe Christ's continuing work and to capture the essence of pastoral leadership. The church was a ship in need of navigation through all sorts of hazards and weather conditions.

Take, for example, these words of Clement of Alexandria:

> The guide is like a navigator directing the ship according to
> the star; prepared to hold himself in readiness for every
> suitable action; accustomed to despise all difficulties and
> dangers when it is necessary to undergo them; never doing
> anything precipitate or incongruous either to himself or the
> common weal; taking thought for the future; and not captive
> to his emotions either in waking hours or in dreams.[3]

Or, even more to the point, take the Clementine Homilies:

> The church is like a great ship carrying through a violent
> storm those from many places, who seek to live in the city of
> the good kingdom. Think of God as the shipmaster. Think of
> Christ as the pilot. If so, then imagine the episcopal officer is
> like a mate, the deacons like sailors, the teacher like a
> midshipman. The passengers are the laity.[4] The world is the
> sea. Temptations, persecutions, and dangers toss the ship
> about like cyclonic winds. Afflictions come in waves. The
> deceivers and false prophets are like uncertain winds and
> squalls. The jagged rocks and promontories await like judges
> in high places threatening terrible sentences. There are wild
> places where two seas meet. These are like unreasonable
> schismatics who doubt of the promises of truth. One must
> beware of pirates, the hypocrites ... If you are going to sail
> with a fair wind so that you will reach the harbour of the
> hoped-for city, pray so as to be heard ... Let those sailing
> expect every tribulation, as travelling over a great and
> troubled sea, the world: sometimes disheartened, persecuted,
> dispersed, hungry, thirsty, naked and hemmed in; at other
> times united, assembled and at rest.[5]

The spiritual gift, then, of the *kybernētēs* was not unfamiliar in
the early church and applied both to Christ and to Christian
leaders.

A recent professional definition of navigation reads like this:
'Navigation is then seen to be the safe conduct of the craft from one

berth to another, and its practice is to ensure that each passage is successfully and expeditiously completed.'[6] In the church, the gift of navigating the people of God consists in charting the course to their destination, and of piloting them through all sorts and conditions of wind, weather, climates, tides, hazards, obstacles, changes and uncertainties safely to their goal.

In the ancient world the exact role of the *kybernētēs* was fluid and depended on the size or nature of the boat being piloted. Sometimes, in a small boat the helmsman, as well as having a hand on the tiller, would be the vessel's owner and captain. In a larger boat the helmsman's role might be specifically limited to that of navigation, and he might, even then, commit the actual task of steering to someone else under his command. In the Roman navy the helmsman might be the commanding officer. In a merchant ship he was usually a professional navigator, hired by the owner, charterer or captain of the ship for a particular voyage.[7] Whatever the differences imposed by the size of the vessel, the essence of the task of the helmsman was always the same: safely to navigate the course of the ship.

The very fluidity of the image makes it particularly appropriate to the pastoral role since that is also very diverse. Some churches are like the small craft that formed the flotilla that crossed the English Channel to evacuate the stranded Allied forces from Dunkirk in June 1940. Pastors in such smaller vessels, have a comprehensive role, but even so must have a clear focus on the overall task of navigation. Other churches are like the stately battleships or luxury liners which dwarf their tiny cousins. In these churches, the structures are necessarily more complex. The role of the navigator may be more specialized. Different churches call for the task of navigation to be handled in different ways. But, whatever the vessel, there is always a need for the gift of the navigator, giving attention to the overall direction of the church and its ministry. Whatever differences there may be, all navigators have a number of characteristics in common, to which we now turn. They are, in no particular order, the need for teamwork, reliability, authority, expertise and versatility, while sensing the weight of responsibility and never losing sight of the destination which is to be reached.

Teamwork

The first characteristic is that the navigator is a member of a team which needs to work harmoniously together if the ship is not to be endangered. He does not usually own the ship, although he may do so. More usually, both in the ancient world and today, the pilot is invited on board for a specific task and then disembarks. He serves the ship's owner and works under the ship's captain. As a hired professional, the pilot or navigator is called upon to advise the master and officers of the ship, but he works under their authority and they retain the responsibility for the safe conduct of the vessel.[8] The 1913 Pilotage Act assumed this, for example, in stipulating that the pilot was liable to a fine if he quitted the ship 'before the service for which he was engaged has been performed and without the consent of the master of the ship'.

Pilots, first of all, then, are not masters and owners but called to serve under the captaincy of another; just as pastors, first and foremost, are called to serve under the command of Jesus Christ and to be obedient to him in all things. It is an obvious point we too easily forget as we frequently confront the temptation to consider that the church *belongs* to us. Faced outright with the accusation, we would, of course, deny it. Our spiritual self-consciousness would never allow us to admit that we think in this way. But we betray ourselves in our speech. We talk of 'my church', 'my people', and even 'my pulpit'. Language, of course, not only expresses how we understand reality but shapes our understanding of reality. So we can easily fall into the trap set by our linguistic shorthand and come to believe that the church really is ours, with the result that God's ownership of the church begins to be supplanted by those of us called merely to pilot it.

The nature of the church is to be 'a people belonging to God' (1 Pet. 2:9) under the one headship or captaincy of the Lord Jesus Christ, and our objective must be to ensure that 'in everything he might have the supremacy' (Col. 1:18). Using a different illustration, but making the same point, Paul wrote of promising the church of Corinth 'to one husband, to Christ, so that I might present you as a pure virgin to him' (2 Cor. 11:2). By this he meant that no human agent, whether Paul himself as a genuine apostle, the false apostles with whom he was doing battle, or well-intentioned and zealous pastors today, must come between the church and Christ. To usurp the place of Christ in the affection and obedience of a church is as criminal as the best man at a wedding stealing the affection and commitment of the bride. It is to betray a trust and fling an honour back in the face of the one who called us.

The success orientation of ministry today encourages the sort of self-assertive leadership which the pilot model, along with other New Testament images, calls into question. But the image of the pilot invites us to examine our motives and discover whether we really do want Christ to be pre-eminent in all things or whether we would like to share some of the glory with him.

A second aspect of teamwork is that, however skilled and professional he (or she) may be, the pilot is called to serve alongside a crew. He does not sail the ship single-handedly. He is part of a team and in that team he plays an important, but circumscribed, role. He serves best when he permits others to do their tasks. He serves least well when he thinks he is omnicompetent. In fact, his service may prove a major liability to others if he seeks to perform every task himself. All this means that, though he may be skilled in particular ways and carry with him delegated authority related to those specialist skills, the pilot must have the ability to form relationships, gain the respect of others and utilize their gifts and skills, allowing the crew to work harmoniously together with him to ensure the safety of the vessel. And those qualities are never more necessary than when the ship is sailing through dangerous waters.

Dependability

The Pilotage Act, quoted above, points out that certain responsibilities have been committed to pilots and they must neither be negligent in fulfilling them nor abdicate their responsibility for them before the time is right. According to this Act, they have no right to leave the ship without the consent of the ship's master. They are called to remain on the bridge as long as they are needed, through all sorts of dangers and difficulties. Indeed, it is probably precisely because there are dangers and difficulties that they were called on board in the first place. Storms and hazards are the essence of the pilot's life. The pilot who wanted to jump ship the moment rocks loomed or gales blew would not be considered worth the title. The pilot must prove reliable.

In a similar way, it is foolish for pastors to expect a smooth ride in ministry, and they need to persevere during periods of storm and difficulty. The passage of the church has had its glorious moments of calm and sunshine, but, for much of its history, it has been in the vortex of inner strife, hostile persecution, inhospitable secularism or massive cultural change. It is during these times that the church has needed pastors to look to, who would stay on the bridge and guide them through. Some, like Dietrich Bonhoeffer, Janani Luwum and Alex Muge, have remained faithful at the cost of their own lives. But their costly perseverance has produced a rich harvest in the lives of others.

The spirit of our age makes it easy to run away. Escape, rather than perseverance, is the more popular option. It is not unknown for pastors today hurriedly to seek a move to waters which they believe will be calmer the moment they run into any difficulty in their church. One senior pastor, with long experience of younger pastors in his care doing just this, suggested to me that many have not been trained to persevere and so give up too easily. Sadly, he reflected, the answer to difficulties today is to walk away from them rather than to work through them. This only produces a style of ministry that achieves nothing except to encourage people to go on running. Would that our commitment to the Lord had the hallmarks of the pilot about it! Then we would stay to guide the church through all sorts of weathers, even barren or stormy ones, until he gave us permission to move.

Authority

While I began by emphasizing the limits of the pilot's role, we cannot avoid the fact that the pilot also carries real authority. True, it is only temporarily delegated by the master or officers, but it is authority none the less. It was for this very reason that the early church frequently resorted to the image. Their fault may well have been to overemphasize this aspect of the image, giving pastors all sorts of biblically unwarranted airs and graces, at the expense of other aspects which build in the checks and balances. But our fault, if anything, is to neglect this aspect of the pilot's role to our detriment.

It is vital that the pilot should exercise authority; the task could not be completed without it. Information has to be exchanged accurately and quickly, and orders given and obeyed promptly. The incident at Teignmouth, mentioned at the beginning of this chapter, is a good illustration of what happens when the pilot's authority is ignored!

To be on a ship adrift in the sea with no-one at the helm is frightening. To use a more contemporary illustration, modern aircraft are increasingly computerized, and the task of the navigator is increasingly redundant. Passengers often feel a trifle uneasy at the thought that there is no human being in control. The old joke about the flight to New York where passengers were greeted with the announcement, 'Welcome aboard, ladies and gentlemen. This is the first fully automated flight to New York. There is no captain or crew in the cockpit. But please relax because nothing can go wrong, go wrong, go wrong …' resonates with the anxieties which lurk not far beneath the surface in most of us.

Pilots are only of use, assuming competence and gift, if they are listened to and allowed to direct. In our current anti-authority climate, where consumer religion reigns, this is not a popular message. But the New Testament is unapologetic about the authoritative role of leaders within the church. 1 Thessalonians 5:12 calls for Christians 'to respect those who work hard among you, who are over you in the Lord and who admonish you'. Hebrews 13:17 sharpens the command further, ordering, 'Obey your leaders and submit to their authority.'

True, neither of these texts, nor the others which speak of authoritative leadership in the church (for example, the frequent references in the pastoral letters), give any support to authoritarianism. Authoritarianism is the abuse of power. Hebrews 13:17 demonstrates a sensitivity to the way in which authority can so easily be abused, and immediately qualifies the invitation to obey leaders by pointing out that 'They keep watch over you as those who must give an account.' Wherever notes of authority are sounded, they are complemented by notes calling on leaders to remember their own vulnerability and accountability together with their need for gentleness and meekness.

Even so, there is an inescapable deposit of teaching in the Bible that God calls some to govern and lead in his church and we should not ignore it. The exercise of authority is inherent in the role of the pilot and is never more in demand than in crisis situations. In recent years many a church would have benefited from recognizing this truth. It might have saved many from the peril of heresy which has caused some churches to be dashed upon a rock. Others might have been saved from drifting aimlessly and achieving nothing in their witness and service from year to year. In Thomas Oden's words,

> The ship in storm does not survive by laborious democratic debate, but by prompt, well-planned action under strict guidance and accountability. Thus a radically populist polity or simplistic equalitarianism where every decision is subjected to popular vote has seldom been regarded as adequate to the mission of this vessel, the church.[9]

Expertise

In Britain the piloting service was set up in 1514, when Henry VIII granted a charter to Trinity House 'for the safe navigation of the Thames because it was considered unwise for young unqualified men to set themselves up as pilots'. It was thought that training and experience were necessary to ensure that people knew what they were doing and that examinations would be a suitable test to prove that the necessary knowledge and skills had been acquired. The matter was taken seriously because the lives of passengers and crew and the safety of boat and cargo were at stake.

It was this point that John Chrysostom called to his aid when, as a young man, he resisted election as a bishop and, at a vital moment in the process, fled. In *On the Priesthood*, he explained his cowardly action:

> If an election to a military dignity was the business in hand, and they who had the right of conferring the honour were to drag forward a brazier, or a shoemaker, or some such artisan,

and entrust the army to his hands, I should not praise the wretched man if he did not take to flight, and do all in his power to avoid plunging into such manifest trouble. If, indeed, it be sufficient to bear the name of pastor, and to take the work in hand haphazard, and there be no danger in this, then, let whoso please accuse me of vainglory; but it behoves one who undertakes this care to have much understanding, and, before understanding, great grace from God and uprightness of conduct, and purity of life and superhuman virtue ...

Moreover, if anyone in charge of a full-sized merchant ship, full of rowers, and laden with a costly freight, were to station me at the helm and bid me cross the Aegean or the Tyrhene sea, I should recoil from the proposal at once: and if anyone should ask me why? I should say. 'Lest I should sink the ship.'[10]

Chrysostom's rationale seems difficult to fault, and yet, in practice, many ignore his argument completely. Often Christians engage in special pleading about the church. They argue that it is different from other organizations and businesses, and so are its leaders. Spiritual gifts, it is said, make training unnecessary. Grace, it is claimed, is what qualifies us to minister, not a paper diploma. The Holy Spirit, it is argued, is the divine teacher and revealer of truth, not a college. So people offer themselves for Christian leadership and seek to steer the ship of the church without any training. Of course, our God is not limited to our normal and human ways of working and, as sovereign Lord, uses and equips whom he will. But, sadly, many who claim to be called and equipped demonstrate ignorance and a lack of skill which are culpable (and which reflect badly on the Holy Spirit who is supposed to have gifted and trained them). The church has frequently suffered in recent decades from the repeating of old heresies, the making of well-worn mistakes and the endless reinventing of the wheel, all because a narrowness of spiritual vision has meant some did not think they needed training.

Rather, with Chrysostom again, it is surely true that the greater the gift the greater the responsibility to train and enhance it.[11] Great gifts need cultivation.

A pilot needs a wide variety of knowledge – knowledge of times and seasons; of tides, weather and winds; of sandbanks, rocks, wrecks and other obstacles; of lights and guidance systems; of how to handle particular vessels and the habits of different types of ship. With knowledge, the pilot can turn these things to his advantage. Without skill these same things can be the means of destruction. It is a common saying among those at sea that 'The navigator who is slave to charts and compass has the freedom of the seas.' As Edward Gibbon put it, 'The wind and the waves are usually on the side of the ablest navigator.'

In the secular world, enormous resources are poured into the training of pilots, and rightly so. Simulators, like the one at Plymouth University, reproduce the experience of entering Dover Harbour at night so that fledgling pilots can learn to interpret the confusing galaxy of lights and bring the ship into harbour safely. Should it be any less so among those who wish to guide the ship of the church?

Think of the knowledge a pastor requires. To pilot the church requires a knowledge of the Lord and his Word; of the church and its ways; of people and their make-up and of the world and its state. Each of these requires at least one discipline in itself. In addition, pastors must have a thorough self-knowledge and have undergone a process of personal spiritual formation with a view to building disciplines and habits of spirituality which will sustain them throughout their ministry and enable them not to crack under pressure. A knowledge of the Bible and its theology, of church history, of pastoral theology and counselling, of communication and preaching, of administration and sociology, to name but a few, are all required. No-one, of course, can hope to master all these, and mastery is not needed. A sufficient knowledge of them, however, is both necessary and possible. On the one hand, this training will prevent costly mistakes from being made and, on the other hand, it will be the means of releasing great spiritual potential and causing the church to mature.

Versatility

Knowledge is one thing; knowing when and how to apply it is

another. The key skill of the pilot is the ability to adapt to changing conditions of the sea – the speed and direction of the wind, the strength and direction of the tide and the changing shape of the sea bed. There are no formulas which will always apply, and there is no room for a rigidity in attitude or the mindless application of unchanging procedures. Intuition plays a role, although the pilot is not a slave to it. Alertness has to be maintained at all times. In a sailing boat there are times when it is necessary to tack to port and others when it is right to tack to starboard, and still others when it is important to keep a steady course. There are times to hoist sails and times to trim them. There are times when it right to weather a storm and times when it is right to run for safe shelter. What is called for is applying what one learned yesterday to the circumstances of today.

I believe the image of the pilot applies most aptly to the work of the pastoral ministry at exactly this point. The task of the pastor is to be at the helm of the church to guide her through the changing conditions in which she worships and serves. No two periods are ever identical.

There are times when the sea is calm and little progress seems to be made. The task then is to discern whether the call of God to his people in such circumstances is to persevere, or whether there are issues that can be addressed which will mean that the becalming influences which have stranded the church can be overcome, enabling her to start to move forward again. There are other times when the storms of persecution rage or the forceful winds of heresy are howling. Then the task is to encourage the church to be faithful to the truth that is in Christ.

There are other times, thank God, when the constructive wind of God's Spirit is blowing, and the task of the pilot is to steer the ship in such a way that she does not break up but rather benefits from all that God is doing. This has been a particular need during recent decades as the successive winds of charismatic renewal and all that followed it have hit us. It has called for a great sensitivity to the Spirit in order to turn the ship in the right direction so that these winds brought lasting life and mobility rather than division and disillusion. Acute awareness of God's Word to teach people truth and challenge excesses, great love for God's people so that fears could be overcome and fleshly enthusiasms restrained, and humble openness to God's ever contemporary Spirit have all been required (but too often absent) to pilot the ship safely.

With the onset of postmodernity, the skill of the pilot is going to be even more necessary in the church. The landmarks with which we have been familiar during the 'modern' period have been removed and the gales of cultural change are blowing fast and furious. The place of grand narratives which helped us to interpret the world, our understanding of reason, our belief in progress, the commitment to integration and even the idea of truth itself are all under review. People, temporarily at least, seem attracted by surface rather than depth, image rather than reality, play rather than purpose, fragmentation rather than coherence, the reader's meaning rather than the author's intent, despair rather than hope.[12] People need help through these uncertain waters. Attempts to cling to the familiar landmarks will fail, since they have been removed. The waters are uncharted as yet. Some argue that the way forward is to reassert vigorously a traditional evangelicalism which was wedded to earlier philosophical frameworks, and believe that by shouting louder their case will be proved. Others believe they must pioneer new directions under trendy titles like 'post-evangelicalism'.[13] Pastors will not have all the answers. But they will be called upon to guide, to be abreast of the wider scene and the currents which have their marked effect.

The pastor must be a spiritual navigator both in terms of the larger church's relation to the general development of culture and with respect to the life of his or her particular local church. Many churches get nowhere because they lack any sense of direction. They merely drift. Someone needs to chart an overall course and guide a church so that it gets somewhere. And that, with all the caveats already mentioned, is the responsibility of the pastor. It needs to be done under the direction of Christ and in full co-operation with fellow leaders and members. But it still needs to be done. It is in order to overcome the malaise which has afflicted so much church life that many have recently found value in framing a mission statement, working on a vision for the future and setting out how their particular church will function to achieve the mission committed to them by their Lord. Providing such policies are neither set in stone, nor imposed upon unwilling congregations, here is a good example of the way in which the pastor should serve as the *kybernētēs* in the local church.

The task of navigating does not end there. It proves essential in particular meetings as well as in terms of the overall direction of the church. In business meetings the church should be open to the leading of God's Spirit and seek to catch the direction in which Jesus Christ would have us go. No mechanism for decision-making, whether dictatorship, democracy or consensus-seeking, exempts us from the need for a pilot in such meetings.

In worship services, too, the gift is necessary. We've all experienced worship that has begun in the Spirit only to degenerate into being everyone's favourite sing-song or to become a platform on which people can voice their political views. John Gunstone put it beautifully when he wrote:

> The gathering is drawn along by the wind of the Spirit, but unless the leader's hand is firmly on the tiller, there is every danger that the ship's course may be deflected by the cross-currents of human emotions and ambition that move not very far below the surface of the sea over which she sails.[14]

If only the church had had more skilled pilots during these decades of evangelical growth and cultural change, perhaps she would have been spared the tragic number of wrecks and mishaps she has experienced. Perhaps, too, it might not have resulted in others, out of fear or obstinacy, casting anchor and refusing to budge an inch in the hope that the wind would pass quickly.

Responsibility

Any ordinary pilot must be aware of the value of the ship, of its cargo and, even more, of the lives of its passengers and crew. The awareness produces a healthy sense of respect for the vessel and the sea. Many acts of heroism can be recounted which have aimed at preventing loss of life and property. But the value of an ordinary vessel, even if fully loaded with cargo and people, is nothing compared with the value of the ship of the church.

Chrysostom, again, pointed out the difference. Having protested that no-one in their right mind would ask him to pilot a merchant ship lest he should sink it, he went on:

> Well, where the loss concerns material wealth, and the danger extends only to bodily death, no one will blame those who exercise great prudence; but where the shipwrecked are destined to fall, not into the ocean, but into the abyss of fire, and the death which awaits them is not that which severs the soul from the body, but one which together with this dismisses it to eternal punishment, shall I incur your wrath and hate because I did not plunge headlong into so great an evil?[15]

The work of the pastor has to do with people – the summit of God's creation. However valuable material possessions may be and however much our society worships the bottom line on a financial statement, materialism has nothing to compare with the value of people. People have an intrinsic value because we are made in the image of God. And that holds even for the person in whom that image has been most damaged. The book of Proverbs reminds us of the need to view people from this perspective, even when they are poor, powerless or at the bottom of the social heap. 'He who oppresses the poor shows contempt for their Maker, but whoever is kind to the needy honours God' (Prov. 14:31; 17:5). Our value as people was further enhanced, if that is possible, when God offered his one and only Son as a ransom for us.

As disciples of Jesus Christ, called to be pilots in his church, we cannot do other than be intensely aware of his compassion for and ministry to people. He reserved his most scathing comments for the religious leaders of his day who were so wrapped up in their concerns about the law that they had lost sight of people and failed to lift their burdens and bring them into the liberty of God's love when they could have done so (Matt. 23:1–39, especially vv. 13–24). Given that our responsibility is, after our responsibility to God himself, first and foremost to people, we must be careful to measure all our activity against this benchmark. God forgive us when the lesser concerns of institutional preservation, empire-building, doctrinal peculiarities or selfish ambition assume a greater priority!

Chrysostom's comment also leads us to the final characteristic of pastoral work which is inherent in the image of the pilot.

Purpose

Implicit in the work of the pilot is the idea of a destination. He is aiming to take a vessel safely into port, or safely out of harbour, or to negotiate some tricky passage without loss or damage. It always involves movement and there is always a goal to be achieved. Everything he does is determined by the desire to reach the destination safely. The pilot is not the captain of a pleasure cruiser, content to sail around the bay in circles, enjoying the warmth of the sun and entertaining passengers with music and drink. He has a job to do, a destination to reach. The pilot who forgets his role would soon be sacked.

Good pastors are supremely conscious of their destination and keep it firmly in mind. Their work is not governed by the here and now, or by short-term goals. They have an eye to the future, to the end of all time when they must give an account not only of their own lives (2 Cor. 5:10) but, in some measure, of their ministries and the people whom God has committed to their charge.

This eschatological motivation, which we have already observed in the image of the builder, has a double thrust to it. It concerns the goal or destination both of the individual believer and of the corporate body of the church. Paul expresses it various ways. 'My dear children, for whom I am again in the pains of childbirth until Christ is formed in you ...' (Gal. 4:19). He keeps his objective clear by speaking of the Lord who 'gave himself up for her [the church] to make her holy, cleansing her by the washing with water through the word, and to present her to himself as a radiant church, without stain or wrinkle or any other blemish, but holy and blameless' (Eph. 5:26–27). He uses every ounce of his God-given energy so that he 'may present everyone perfect in Christ' (Col. 1:28–29). Or, to refer again to his image of the bride, he longs to present the church 'as a pure virgin to him' (2 Cor. 11:2). All Paul's pastoral work is determined by the destiny of the people of God and the need to prepare them for that final meeting with their God and Saviour.

Would that it were so today! The loss of the sense of the eternal in the church and the (perhaps) over-preoccupation with the things of this world have muted the sense of responsibility which arises from having a heavenward orientation. Without this future focus the cry for justice and peace – great biblical themes – too easily become a quest for mere material comfort or political progress. Too many pastors have exchanged the role of the pilot for the role of the captain of the pleasure cruiser, and have lost a sense of direction and accountability. Our task is not to be popular, or to keep the passengers happy, but to make them holy. Anything less involves a desertion of the bridge and a dereliction of our duty.

In making the point, we need to reflect on the fact that the destiny of the pilot is closely bound up with that of the ship he is piloting. The ship sinks and the pilot goes down with her. She reaches the safety of the harbour and the pilot does too. Paul was certainly conscious of the same point (1 Cor. 9:27; 2 Cor. 5:10–14). The last thing he wanted to have done was to have laboured in vain and to have missed out on eternal reward because he had been negligent in sailing the ship of the church safely to its eternal destination.

Conclusion

Pastors will not have every spiritual gift, but the gift of the *kybernētēs* seems to lie at the heart of the pastoral calling. The other gifts of counselling, evangelism, teaching or prophecy will revolve around this one. It reminds us that our duty is not only to individuals but also to the corporate vessel of the church, to enable the church to negotiate the hazards of this life and the winds that threaten to break her up, guiding the ship safely into the eternal harbour. It takes both gift and skill to know just what touch to have upon the tiller – when to be firm and when to be gentle, when to be authoritative and when to let go, when to be proactive and when to be passive, when to be assertive and when to give others more responsibility. But that is the calling for which Jesus Christ equips some with the gift of pastoring, while he himself remains the supreme pilot in whose hands all lesser navigators are safe.

Questions for reflection

1. Let me examine the language I use to talk of the church in which I serve as a pastoral leader. Does it indicate that I think I own the church? What does it say about my motives and attitudes? Can I genuinely say that God owns the church?

2. As a person under authority, how do I interpret the difficulties I face? Are they genuinely signs of God saying, 'It's time to move on'? Or is God really wanting me to stay and work through the stormy patch?

3. Am I afraid to exercise a God-given authority which is inherent in my calling? If not, am I alert to the possible abuse of authority which has caused many to fall? Is my conscience clear before God that my authority is being used in the manner of Christ?

4. In reflecting on the training I received for ministry, was it an adequate preparation even for where I am today? Is there need for a refresher course or retraining at this juncture?

5. In assessing my practice of ministry, am I aware that I am being versatile and sensitive to the winds of the Spirit, or is it rather a case of endlessly repeating the same formulae and going through the routines and motions as I have done for years?

6. Do I still love people, or have I wearied of them? Are they still, to me, the most precious cargo I could ever be called upon to conduct on a journey?

7. To what extent is my current ministry shaped by a sense of my need to prepare God's people for their eternal judgment and destiny?

7
Scum

'... we have become the
scum of the earth' (1 Cor. 4:13).

It is the most unflattering, the most uncomfortable of images. Paul
speaks of himself and Apollos as 'the scum of the earth, the refuse of
the world' (1 Cor. 4:13). These are not nice phrases to apply to
anyone, even oneself. In courteous religious circles such language
would surely be condemned as 'un-Christlike'. None would dare to
voice such negative opinions, especially of their pastors!
Disconcerting verses like these are usually just ignored. So why
haven't we done the same? Recalling the famous answer given by the
mountaineer when asked, 'Why climb Everest?', the reply is simply,
'Because it's there.' Since it is included in inspired Scripture, some
sense should be made of it.

Paul uses two words to describe himself in this most shocking of
ways: *perikatharmata* and *peripsēma*. They are closely related, and
conjure up a powerful image even if they do not admit to precise
definition. They both have to do with removing dirt by scrubbing
clean or scouring. It might be to do with scouring dirt from a burnt
pan in the kitchen, cleaning filth from a vegetable or piece of fruit,
or removing uncleanness from the body. The words then came to
stand for the muck which was removed. So it is rightly translated as

off-scourings, dirt, trash, garbage, rubbish, filth, scrapings, sweepings or waste. Eugene Peterson imaginatively translates the verse, 'We're treated like garbage, potato peelings from the culture's kitchen.'[1] The simple point is that however you choose to translate the word there is no polite way of putting it.

Beyond this, as we shall see more fully a little later, the words came to describe the dregs of society, the worthless ones, the no-hopers, the criminals, the vermin and the ne'er-do-wells. Some years ago a violent and disturbing film was produced about a youth prison, inhabited on the one hand by sad young men who were out to get violent revenge wherever they could, and equally savage officers who could scarcely be distinguished from them. The storyline focused on a riot which ensued from their totally dysfunctional personalities and relationships. The film was fittingly called *Scum*. Its horrifying scenes were calculated to traumatize those who saw it. But its ethos captured something of the despair and horror of the way we use the word 'scum' when applied to human beings.

Why is Paul happy to degrade himself in this way and associate himself, as an apostle of Christ, with the dregs of society? The usual answer is to say that he did not really mean it and that he was merely resorting to irony as a way of undermining the boasting of the Corinthian church. It is true that his comment is ironic. But we should not be so quick to leave the matter there, since Paul is also, at the same time, teaching something deep about the nature of Christian ministry.

The Roman culture in which Paul and the Corinthians lived was preoccupied with the pursuit of honour and the avoidance of shame. Honour had to do with one's self-worth, with the way others recognized one's worth and with one's social standing and reputation. It could be ascribed through birth or family connections or acquired and actively sought by playing the game of social climbing. The competition to gain honour was fierce. If honour was affronted it would be vigorously defended. If one chose to ignore a slight it would result in dishonour. The honour of a group took its cue from the honour rating of its leader. They lived in a world where honour was constantly being challenged and where effective responses had to be mounted. Bruce Malina has commented on how much Paul's culture was riddled with this quest for honour:

> ... in the first-century Mediterranean world, every social interaction that takes place outside one's family or outside one's circle of friends was perceived as a challenge to honour, a mutual attempt to acquire honour from one's social equal. Thus gift-giving, invitations to dinner, debates over issues of law, buying and selling, arranging marriages, arranging what we might call cooperative ventures for farming, business, fishing, mutual help, and the like – all these sorts of interaction take place according to the pattern of honour called challenge-response.[2]

The Corinthians had certainly drunk deeply at the Roman cultural well and imbibed the value of honour into their bloodstream. They wanted to be rich, powerful, knowledgeable, filled, wise, strong, sophisticated, and so honoured (see 1 Cor. 4:8). And, naturally, they wanted their leaders to be the same (1 Cor. 3:1–4). How else would they be respected?

Paul refuses to play their game. Christian values are radically different, and Christian leaders must be judged, and judge themselves, by equally different values. They, and we, must counter the culture in which we live, not baptize it with a slight sprinkling of Christian folk religion.

Paul does this as he speaks of his feelings about his ministry (1 Cor. 4:9–13). How different he is from the well-healed and comfortable Corinthians! As a minister of Christ he feels rather like a condemned man being marched into an arena to face death at the hands of some wild beast or undefeatable gladiator who will tear him limb from limb while spectators in the crowded stadium look on and applaud (v. 9). This shameful and degrading spectacle, he argues, is no accident but part of God's design. Having set out his feelings about the experience of ministry, he next sets out the facts. While the Corinthians enjoy their secure position and desirable relationship with their society, he experiences shame, hunger, thirst, poverty, homelessness, scorn, persecution and slander (vv. 10–12). It is this that leads to his conclusion that he is 'the scum of the earth, the refuse of the world'.

Pastors, in their lowest moments, might well feel they can identify with Paul. From time to time conflicts within the church and opposition from the world might give us an inkling of Paul's experience. But, by any objective measurement, the vast majority of pastors in the West know very little of such ministry. Elsewhere it may be different. In many places pastors have literally experienced all that Paul mentions for the sake of the gospel. But in the West it is unlikely to be so. This leads us to ask whether what Paul is writing here is limited to his apostolic role, and therefore is irrelevant to us, or whether it does have wider implications for pastoral ministry. Since we happily apply the remainder of his argument in chapters 1 – 4 to contemporary ministry, and the argument is seamless, it would surely not be right to excise this one statement and say it does not apply. If we are happy to consider ourselves as servants, gardeners, builders and even fools for Christ, then why not scum and refuse?

If it does apply to those who stand in the tradition of Paul as pastoral leaders within the church, what does it mean? Three themes emerge.

Ministry as contemptible

Descriptions like 'scum' and 'refuse' were used metaphorically for anything which was contemptible, and, according to the normal values of Paul's culture, being a servant of the gospel was just that. The message of the cross was a nonsense in the 'real world' of economic power, political authority, military capability and commercial mastery. How could the cross possibly be powerful or even relevant? And the values that flowed from the cross, those of humility, weakness and suffering, were just as despised in a world which placed value on pride, strength and health.

What was true of Paul's culture remains true of our own, if not more so.

I remember a schoolmaster of mine making it plain to my parents that for me to enter ministry was a 'waste of a life'. There are so many more useful and productive things that can be done. More money could have been earned in other ways; more good could have been achieved by becoming a social worker; more use could have been made of gifts by training as an academic; more influence could be wrought by being a politician ... or so he thought. But to be a messenger of a man who was crucified was sheer waste – or, in other words, refuse that you throw away. Society doesn't credit ministers of the gospel, at least these days, with much prestige – unless one is a bishop or archbishop, that is, and then one has all the right connections. The way ministers are portrayed on TV, usually as ineffectual wimps or bumbling buffoons, is a symptom of how most people really think.

Even more significant than any personal implications for a minister of the gospel is what this says about the conflict of values between the gospel and the world. The world values beautiful people, who wear designer clothes, who are financially well off and who know their way around. It is a Vanity Fair of a world. But the gospel, epitomized by the cross, is about those things which it despises. The crucified Lord 'had no beauty or majesty to attract us to him' (Is. 53:2); 'did not open his mouth' to defend himself or his honour (Is. 53:7); was stripped of any clothing; and seemed a naïve beginner, a helpless pawn in a game of power politics he didn't understand. He was, in the other sense of the word, an 'innocent' victim. The cross, then, is bound to generate serious conflict with a society which is addicted to an opposite set of values. And servants of the cross will inevitably be caught in the crossfire.

Typical of the values of the chattering classes, who have such a determining influence on our society through their writing or broadcasting, is the mocking article of Julie Burchill which appeared in the *Sunday Times* in 1984. It expressed great amusement that anyone still believed 'the blatant lies the Bible is composed of'. 'Even the Ten Commandments,' she wrote, 'which otherwise quite discerning people get all misty-eyed about, are prehistoric and unfeasible.' Then, dismissing all, one by one, except 'Thou shalt not kill', she concluded that 'a practising Christian is only slightly more acceptable than a transvestite'. The conflict of values is real!

The sad truth, however, is that the conflict is not always between the church on the one side and the world on the other. Much of the friction will be felt within the church itself. Contemporary Christians may be just as deeply contaminated by their culture's value-system as the Corinthians were. Even those who are not deeply enmeshed in social networks which espouse the world's values are exposed to them through the television and other mass media. It is hard to maintain the integrity of a Christian value system when the opposite is so pervasive.

Pastors are not necessarily any more exempt from the pressure to conform to the world's mindset than others, although, by their very calling as proclaimers of the cross, they should, perhaps, be more aware of the problem. So pastors must be alert to the tensions and seductions. They must be prepared for the opprobrium which their message will attract. And, in the face of all cultural despisers of the cross, they must engage in bold teaching which spells out its implications with increasing clarity and calls the church to accept ridicule.

Ministry as sacrifice

Several commentators suggest that the image of scum has more to it than we have yet suggested. C. K. Barrett translates the word *perikatharmata* as 'scapegoat'.[3] He does so because in later writings the word was used to refer to the Greek idea of catharsis. Cities would sacrifice some unfortunate person to the gods, especially to Artemis, Apollo, Poseidon and Athena, in order to ward off disaster. The sacrifice was supposed to appease the gods and the catastrophe be averted. The human sacrifice would act as a sort of cleansing agent, scrubbing off the dirt which had caused offence to the divinities.[4]

Paul was cautious about speaking of his own ministry in sacrificial terms. He would never have considered that his ministry effected redemption in the lives of his hearers. That was achieved through the sacrifice of Jesus Christ alone. And yet he saw all Christian living as a call to sacrifice (Rom 12:1; 15:16), and he placed his own ministry within a sacrificial framework. He wrote to the Philippians that he was 'being poured out like a drink offering on the sacrifice and service coming from your faith' (2:17). He used the same figure of speech to speak of his death in 2 Timothy 4:6. To the Corinthians he said that 'death is at work in us, but life is at work in you' (2 Cor. 4:12).

The simple point is that sacrificial victims wasted their lives in order that others might have the benefit of life. If that is what people considered Paul to be doing – throwing his life away as if it were some trash to be disposed of – so be it. But good would flow into the lives of others as a result, in true sacrificial fashion. Far from being a title of shame, 'the scum of the earth, the refuse of the world' is a description of which he could be proud. It meant he was caught up in the sacrificial process which would bring life to others by his preaching of the gospel.

The image then calls us to question our approach to ministry at its deepest level. How much do we see ministry in sacrificial terms, with ourselves as the sacrificial victim? In a devastating critique of much contemporary ministry, riddled as it is by personality cults and fuelled by the temptations of big entertainment events, my colleague, Meic Pearse, has observed that so much ministry is a highly self-conscious exercise in feeding our own egos, rather than feeding Christ's lambs. He issues this challenge:

> What is certain is that we cannot really serve as long as we are thinking about ourselves. In the modern West, however, we inhabit a culture of narcissism in which everything – education, TV, magazines, advertisements – teaches us to improve our social status and the feelings we have about ourselves and others about us. Our activities are simply means and techniques (and, oh, how we love techniques!) to that end ... As a result, we have ministry-superstars. Attention and limelight are focused upon *them*, rather than upon the service they are allegedly performing – or what is more to the point – upon Jesus, whose badge they own.[5]

Certainly, in the eyes of many, the contemporary practice of ministry serves to ensure that pastors would never merit the title of 'scum of the earth'. Sacrifice, in any meaningful sense, doesn't come into the picture.

Ministry as participation

There is another facet to this image of ministry as throwing one's life away for the benefit of others. If Paul was not himself the redemptive sacrifice, his suffering brought him closer to the one who was.

The beautiful people of the church at Corinth would have had no wish to accept suffering as part of the Christian experience. To them, suffering would have been an embarrassment, since the coming of Christ, in their minds, meant that the new age could be experienced now in all its fullness.[6] The normal conventions of this world no longer applied to them; they could live continuously in the realm of the supernatural and leave the natural world behind. The resurrection was past (15:12). To them, the future had fully and finally arrived. Suffering, together with other limitations of the body and of custom, belonged to the old age and so no longer had any hold on the Christian.

But Paul points out that 'up to this moment' (4:13) he continues to suffer, to be hungry and to receive rough treatment. True, the new age had been set in motion, but it had not yet been fully implemented. It was already here but not yet fully consummated. To live as if it had been was to live a costly illusion. The believer's lot was to live between times. The consummation of the kingdom to which they looked forward was certainly to have an impact on the way they lived in their 'now'. But equally they were to live with the realities of the world around them.

One such reality was that suffering was to remain a part of Christian experience until the trumpet sounded and death itself was swallowed up in victory (15:51–56). We should not consider this an unfortunate side-effect of some neat but deficient plan of salvation. It is an integral aspect of the plan of salvation which rests on the humiliating death of Christ. Those who believe in Christ were to identify with him by experiencing the tension in their lives of knowing the pain of his suffering *and* the triumph of his resurrection. Theirs was simultaneously to be a theology of the cross and a theology of glory. The one without the other would not be fully Christian.

In response to the false imbalance of the Corinthian theology, then, Paul stresses that suffering is a mark of authentic Christian experience and, furthermore, that it has value in bringing the believer into closer relationship with his or her Lord. How else can we identify with a crucified Lord except by entering into his suffering?

What is true of every believer is especially true of those called on to preach the gospel of the cross. 'We always carry around in our body the death of Jesus, so that the life of Jesus may also be revealed in our body' (2 Cor. 4:10). 'I want to know Christ and the power of his resurrection and the fellowship of sharing in his sufferings, becoming like him in his death, and so, somehow, to attain to the resurrection from the dead' (Phil. 3:10–11). 'Now, I rejoice in what was suffered for you, and I fill up in my flesh what is still lacking in regard to Christ's afflictions for the sake of his body, which is the church' (Col. 1:24).[7] These Paul asserts unashamedly are the authentic marks of a minister of Jesus Christ.

It is with these verses in mind that D. A. Carson warns those in leadership, or aspiring to it, that

> Leaders in the church should suffer most. They are not like generals in the military who stay behind the lines. They are the assault troops, the front-line people, who lead by example as much as by word. To praise a form of leadership that despises suffering is therefore to deny the faith.[8]

Since we continue to live in the in-between time, we continue to know the mixture in our experience of sometimes identifying with Christ's death and sometimes knowing the power of his resurrection. All the ups and downs of ministry are for us, as for Paul, events in which we can join with Jesus in his dying and rising. Neither has a priority, but neither must be omitted.

Ministry will often have the feel of Calvary about it. The darkness, the despair, the hiddenness of God, the awfulness of desertion, the powerlessness of it, the weakness we feel – all these aspects are 'illuminated by the cross'.[9] But we experience these as people who view them from the other side of Calvary, from the standpoint of those who stand beside an empty tomb. That tells us that what the world regards as folly is in fact wisdom; weakness is strength; darkness leads to light and death is the way to life.

Conclusion

If this is what it means to be 'the scum of the earth and the refuse of the world', then surely, without making light of the cost involved, we shall not only welcome the title and put up with the abuse and shame implied, but gladly embrace the experience and bear the pain of being a sacrifice so that others might live. For, surely, we shall want to be true ministers of Christ, not charlatans; and to be that, we need to enter into his experience. Luther was right: 'The cross puts everything to the test.'[10]

Questions for reflection

1. How far am I status-conscious? To what extent do I find myself wanting to defend my honour in ministry? Is my reaction consistent with Paul or in opposition to him?

2. Have people told me that pastoral ministry is a waste of my life and my gifts? What do I genuinely feel, deep down, about such comments?

3. How much has the value-system of the world infiltrated the church where I minister? How seriously do I take the conflict between the value system of the world and that of the cross? How much do I teach about it and help people to understand?

4. Paul describes his ministry in a number of different ways using language associated with sacrifice. What place does sacrifice have in my understanding of ministry?

5. Where do I stand in the 'already'/'not yet' dimensions of the kingdom? Am I truly balanced or do I overbalance on one side at the expense of the other? What about the people I lead? What steps can I take to ensure that a biblical balance is maintained?

6. How much do I see the ups and downs of my ministry as identifying with the dying and rising of Jesus?

7. To what extent do I really believe that the image of scum and refuse is appropriate to contemporary ministry? Or may I dismiss it quickly?

8
Shepherd

'Be shepherds of the church
of God ...' (Acts 20:28).

The most popular image for the work of the ministry is that of the
shepherd. It is, as Thomas Oden has described it, the 'pivotal
analogy' of ministry.[1] Its popularity means that it is likely to suffer
from two opposing disadvantages. On the one hand, it is so familiar
that we take it for granted and do not give any serious consideration
to its depth. On the other hand, we are so accustomed to it that it is
difficult to say anything new about it. It is a comprehensive image
and it makes a fitting conclusion to our consideration of other New
Testament images of ministry. In this concluding chapter we seek to
stand back and take a panoramic view of the shepherd which will
involve our criss-crossing back and forth over the Bible to see the
way it uses the metaphor.[2]

The word is used only four times in the New Testament, once as
a noun and three times in a verbal form, to describe the work of
pastoral leaders in the church. Jesus commissions Peter to 'Take care
of my sheep' (John 21:16). Paul warns the Ephesian elders, 'Keep
watch over yourselves and all the flock of which the Holy Spirit has
made you overseers. Be shepherds of the church of God, which he
bought with his own blood' (Acts 20:28). Peter, similarly, commis-

sions the elders to 'Be shepherds of God's flock that is under your care, serving as overseers – not because you must, but because you are willing, as God wants you to be; not greedy for money, but eager to serve' (1 Pet. 5:2). In Ephesians, pastors (shepherds) are mentioned as a gift of the ascended Lord to his church alongside teachers. Their work is 'to prepare God's people for works of service, so that the body of Christ may be built up' (4:11–12).

These explicit references by no means exhaust the image. Only by standing back and considering the total sweep of Scripture can we understand what these brief references mean. Once we do that we find an image which is both frequent and multi-dimensional. Given the whole picture, seven polarities can be identified as a means to exploring the image in some depth.

God and Israel

Israel's divine shepherd

The image was a natural one for Israel to adopt both as a description of their God and of their own human leaders. They belonged to a pastoral economy and the role of the shepherd was fundamental to their existence. The dryness of the land they inhabited meant that shepherds were always on the move, leading their sheep in search of new and fresh pastures. Among the peoples of the ancient Near East the title of 'shepherd' was commonly applied to their kings and rulers. It was viewed as a role which required the exercise of real authority. It is for this reason that Psalm 78:70–72 refers to David as 'the shepherd of his people Israel'. An echo of the shepherd's authority can be heard, too, in the 'Shepherd's Psalm', where we are reminded that shepherds carry not only a staff to comfort but a rod to rule as well. For all this, in the Old Testament, the title is essentially assigned to God.

The idea that God was the shepherd of his people was embedded in the living piety of Israel. Jacob, reflecting on his long life, turned naturally to the image and spoke of 'the God who has been my shepherd all my life to this day' (Gen. 48:15). He went on to attribute the cause of Joseph's fruitfulness to 'the hand of the Mighty One of Jacob, because of the Shepherd, the Rock of Israel, because of your father's God, who helps you, because of the Almighty, who blesses you' (Gen. 49:24–25).

The stress throughout was on the leadership, provision and guidance offered by God as their shepherd (see, for example, Pss. 23:3; 68:7 and Jer. 50:19). The image always came to the fore when the people of God were on the move. In the wilderness they were not to be 'like sheep without a shepherd' (Num. 27:17; see also Ps. 78:52–53). Similarly, in declaring the nightmare of the exile over, God showed himself to be the one who 'tends his flock like a shepherd: He gathers the lambs in his arms and carries them close to his heart; he gently leads those that have young' (Is. 40:11).

With a shepherd, David, as King of Israel it is not surprising, too, that the devotional literature of Israel, as reflected in the Psalms, should abound in pastoral imagery. In doing so, it was not ascribing a formal title to God but giving expression to a warm and close, although respectful and dependent, relationship. It gives rise to praise, exultation, petition and prayer. The image was sufficiently broad to encompass both the blessed and comforting side of their experience (for example, Pss. 28:9; 95:7; 100:3; 121:4) and also its tough and terrifying aspects (for example, Pss. 44:11, 22; 80:1). Whether their experience was one of darkness or light, of shadow or sunshine, of failure or success, they were glad to affirm that they were the flock under the care and direction of the great Shepherd of Israel, and to him belonged praise for ever (Ps. 79:13).

Israel's human shepherds

In spite of its obvious suitability for David, Israel was reticent to use the title for their earthly king. Their reluctance to do so was probably a reaction to the way in which their pagan neighbours regularly referred to their kings as shepherds.[3] Nevertheless, the image was used frequently by the prophets in a negative sense, to describe the failures of human leadership. The policies of both political and priestly leaders had led the children of Israel to disaster; making light, as they did, of the terms of the covenant. These policies not only permitted but positively encouraged the people to wander astray and drift down the path of spiritual adultery. As time went by without any corrective action being taken, the sheep gathered speed until nothing could prevent them from rushing headlong over the precipice into the exile.

The prophets Jeremiah, Ezekiel and Zechariah condemn the recklessness of these human shepherds most clearly. Jeremiah calls them senseless and says their fault was that they did not enquire of the LORD (10:21). Rather than protecting the flock, they destroyed it and scattered the sheep (23:1–5). Under these foolish leaders the sheep became lost, left to roam and wander over the hills without any sense of where their true home was (50:6).

Ezekiel's indictment is even more severe. He accuses the shepherds not just of negligence but of deliberately killing the sheep so that they might themselves benefit from the wool and meat thereby acquired. In a crucial saying, Ezekiel charged them with failing in their duty of caring for the sheep. 'You have not strengthened the weak or healed the sick or bound up the injured. You have not brought back the strays or searched for the lost' (34:4). They had, instead, ruled brutally. As a result the flock had been scattered and destroyed.

Zechariah is just as damning. Shepherds speak comfortable words, but the words are sheer deceit (10:3). They, again, fail to protect the sheep. Instead, they willingly send them on their way to slaughter in order to line their own pockets (11:4–6).

God's verdict on these culpable and negligent shepherds is severe. His anger 'burns' against them (Zech. 10:3). They will be driven away without any possibility of escape (Jer. 22:22; 25:34). They will be slaughtered, without mercy, just as they have slaughtered those they should have been protecting (Jer. 25:34). So God will remove them from caring for the flock, cut off their means of support, and hold them accountable for all the wickedness they have done (Ezek. 34:7–10). The covenant love of God cannot permit his people to be ruined in this way; consequently, he, himself, will directly assume the role of Shepherd of Israel (Ezek. 34:11–31; Zech. 10:43). In doing so, he will restore peace and justice to his people, remedy their hurts and reinstate them in rich, green pasture land.

God's delegation, to human leaders, of the work of leading, protecting and guiding Israel ended in momentous failure. It was a risk too far. Human shepherds had been unable to resist the temptations inherent in their role and so had abused both their power and their sheep. This shameful passage in Israel's history makes it even more remarkable that God was ever again prepared, in some measure, to trust the leadership of his church to 'under-shepherds'. It makes it the responsibility of all of us who serve as shepherds in the church today to learn the lessons of this earlier disaster diligently in order that we might not fall into the same temptations. The abuse of power and privilege, speaking our own words while claiming them to be the word of God, and spiritual indifference which allows the sheep to stray down dangerous paths, remain potent temptations which trap many pastors. We need to take whatever steps are necessary to ensure that we do not join the list of false shepherds.

Jesus and us

The metaphor of the shepherd continues to enjoy lively currency in the New Testament in reference to both divine and human leaders. Jesus speaks of himself as the good shepherd, and is spoken of by others as the great shepherd, while the Holy Spirit provides 'under-shepherds' for his church.

The good shepherd

When Jesus spoke of himself as a shepherd it was not surprising that he needed to qualify the claim with the word 'good'. Shepherds had a dubious reputation by his time. They were judged to be constitutionally dishonest. People were forbidden to buy anything from them because it was bound to have been stolen. They were not accepted as witnesses in court because they would almost certainly be unreliable. Furthermore, their lifestyle prevented them from worshipping regularly at the temple, so they were considered to be among the unclean. They were listed among those who practised a despised trade. Shepherds were stigmatized. They were not good role models.

The adoption, then, of the title 'good shepherd' by Jesus is remarkable. The scholar Joachim Jeremias has stated that the favourable picture of the shepherd which we are given in Jesus' teaching is quite isolated.[4] In rabbinic literature in general there are only unfavourable references to herdsmen.

Jesus is clearly staking a messianic claim to be the true shepherd of Israel and thus to be fulfilling the prophecies of Ezekiel and Zechariah that God would shepherd his people himself. At the same time, however, he has to distance himself from the popular image the crowd would have of shepherds.

In what does the goodness of Jesus, as the good shepherd, consist? John 10:1–18 provides us with a complex answer. First, he is good because there is a close personal relationship between the shepherd and his flock. He knows them by name, and they follow him because they know his voice (vv. 3–4). He is no stranger to them (v. 5). Secondly, as the gate of the sheep, he is good because he provides security, salvation and pasture for them (vv. 7–10). Thirdly, and supremely, he is the good shepherd because he 'lays down his life for the sheep' (vv. 11, 15, 17–18). This is not the way a hired hand would behave. When a wild animal comes to harry the sheep, the hired hand protects his own life first and runs away. The hired hand prefers to sacrifice the lives of the sheep rather than his own. But Jesus sacrifices his own life in order to preserve the lives of the sheep. Many, hearing this, would have recalled the way in which the false prophets laid down the lives of the sheep for those of the shepherds. Jesus reverses all their pretentious falsehood. Fourthly, while the false shepherds were constantly accused of scattering the sheep, the role of the good shepherd is to gather the sheep, even those from other pens, and unite them into one flock (v. 16).

This concept of the good shepherd, not surprisingly, was taken up and developed by later New Testament writers as they reflected on the ministry of Jesus. According to Hebrews he is the 'great Shepherd of the sheep' who through the shedding of his blood continues to equip his flock for doing the father's will (13:20–21). Peter, likewise, acknowledges Jesus as 'the Chief Shepherd' (1 Peter 5:4), who not only oversees the souls of his people on earth (2:24) but serves as an example to those who carry on his work under his authority.

The book of Revelation puts another spin on the image. Here, the shepherd is, paradoxically, a Lamb (7:17).[5] This lamb is anything but feeble, though he has been sacrificed and his blood shed. The lamb is a warrior lamb; the lamb who is at one and the same time the Lion of the tribe of Judah (5:5–6). Once slain, he now was at the centre of power (5:6; 7:17). The task of this shepherd-lamb, reminiscent of Psalm 23:2, is to lead his people through conflict and turmoil to 'springs of living water'.

The under-shepherds

Peter describes Jesus as 'the Chief Shepherd' (1 Pet. 5:4) but recognizes the importance of the place of those who serve as ordinary shepherds of God's flock under his direction. Shepherds, moulded in his image, will give their service freely and without any hint of domination or superiority (1 Pet. 5:2–3). The example to be followed is that of the one who 'lays down his life for the sheep'. John tells us that the natural implication of that for every Christian, but especially for those who are in leadership, is that 'we ought to lay down our lives for one another' (1 John 3:16). Giving, not taking, must be characteristic of our leadership style. Sacrificing ourselves, not sacrificing our sheep, must be what typifies us. Fighting for them, in the face of anything which would destroy them, not fleeing from them, is what is true to the example of Jesus. Gathering and protecting, rather than scattering and wounding, form the trademark of the true shepherd. If his signature is to be written on our ministries, then we shall be living out the script of the good shepherd.

Serving the Chief Shepherd also means that under-shepherds are answerable to him. Under-shepherds are not free agents who can rule the flock as they like. They are accountable servants who will one day have to deliver themselves for assessment. How they treat the flock, then, has eternal, not just temporal, consequences. Peter encourages the elders of his day to imitate the silent suffering of Christ in order that one day they may 'receive the crown of glory that will never fade away' (1 Pet. 5:4).

Tough but tender

Urbanized western human beings, who have little to do with sheep farming, probably have an over-sentimentalized view of the image of the shepherd. We love to see the tiny lambs frolicking in the fields at Easter time, and delight in the warm images their woolly coats summon up in our imaginations, as we're counting them in an attempt to get to sleep. But being a shepherd is not for the faint-hearted. John Stott sheds light on one aspect of the shepherd's unpleasant role. In commenting on Paul's address to the Ephesian elders, he writes, 'For sheep are not at all the clean and cuddly creatures they may appear. In fact they are dirty, subject to unpleasant pests, and regularly need to be dipped in strong chemicals to rid them of lice, ticks and worms. They are also unintelligent, wayward and obstinate.' Wisely, he adds, 'I hesitate to apply the metaphor too closely and characterize the people of God as dirty, lazy or stupid. But some people are a great trial to their pastors (and *vice versa*). And their pastors will persevere in caring for them only if they remember how valuable they are in God's sight.'[6] But his description of working with these obstinate and wayward animals only begins to describe the difficulty of the role which the ancient shepherd would have undertaken.

Toughness

The role of the shepherd today remains demanding and unpleasant. It often calls for long hours, in all weather conditions, and demands great physical perseverance. Even so, the role today is sanitized in comparison to what it was in the ancient world. Alastair Campbell has emphasized the toughness of the work in ancient Israel. It was a demanding occupation because of the very hot climate. It was often necessary to go a great distance from home and to be absent from family for a lengthy time in search of scarce green pasture. It was a hazardous occupation where wild beasts would pounce and unwelcome strangers would be encountered. On many occasions it meant entering 'the valley of the shadow'. It was not all basking in the sunshine. And all this was in addition to the skill needed in keeping the sheep together in a flock, recognizing and curing their diseases and rescuing any strays that got into difficulty. It was no easy task. Campbell's judgment is probably right: 'His unsettled and dangerous life makes him a slightly ambiguous figure – more perhaps like the cowboy of the "Wild West" than the modern shepherd in a settled farming community.'[7] Reality insists that the pleasant picture of the shepherd leading his flock out of town as they follow obediently behind him, like well-drilled schoolchildren holding hands in twos, be rejected in favour of a tougher picture of the shepherd as more akin to a rough frontiersman.

Parallels with contemporary ministry have to be drawn with care, since all metaphors have their limits, and drawing comparisons at the wrong point can be very misleading. And yet some comparisons may be drawn. The work of the pastor can be tough both because of its loneliness and because the pastor is called to enter the valley of the shadow with many of his or her flock. The quiet vigil at the bedside of the terminally ill; plunging with people into the darkness of sudden and unexpected bereavement or tragedy; walking with them through the shadows caused by suffering; standing with them in the apparently impenetrable gloom of depression; sitting with them as they wrestle with the unanswerable question, 'Why me, Lord?', and listening to them as they give voice to the gathering mists of doubt – all these belong to the privilege yet demand of ministry. They take their emotional and spiritual toll. Toughness is required.

The valley of the shadow takes many forms and the pastor is frequently called upon to journey through it with others. The shadows are real and frightening. The rocks hide potential enemies and the nooks and crannies potentially hostile animals. The sun doesn't penetrate directly. It's cold in the valley. To journey through requires not only good self-understanding and self-security, since bearing the burdens of others can often confront the pastor with his or her own unresolved fears and questions, but also a special measure of the grace of God. Only the person of faith, the one who believes that God's love never fails, can journey into the valley knowing that it is a transitional stage of life and not a terminus. A friend of mine preached at the funeral of one of the children killed in the awful tragedy of Aberfan when, in October 1966, 116 children and twenty-eight adults died as a slag heap engulfed their school. A loquacious evangelist, he is not normally deterred by much. But he commented that on that occasion all he could do was emphasize that even though we walk *through* the valley of the shadow of death, we need fear no evil, for God is with us. The valley is a transition, not a terminus.

A second reason why shepherds need to be tough is mentioned by Paul in his address to the Ephesian elders. The sheep are always in danger and it is the shepherd's role to protect them. In ignorance, they may not always appreciate what the shepherd is doing, but it is the shepherd's responsibility nevertheless to defend them. Sometimes it may involve protecting them from themselves as, in the course of a normal day, they pick up the pests and diseases which abound in the sheep's woollen coats. More often it will be the need to provide protection from the wolves and other fierce animals which are waiting to pounce and devour the sheep.

This language may sound alarmist. But it is, in fact, realistic. The preying beasts still prowl. When Paul spoke of savage wolves he had false teachers in mind – successors to the false prophets of the Old Testament – who would divide and destroy the church. The pastor who is formed in the image of the good shepherd will not be complacent about the orthodoxy of what is taught. Erroneous teaching thrives, both among so-called leaders in the church and among academics who train leaders for the church. Indeed, given our contemporary culture's addiction to novelty, heresy is inevitable and even frequently prized as a sacred vessel on the altar of originality.[8] But true pastors are those who keep to the pattern of sound teaching delivered by the apostles and 'contend for the faith that was once for all entrusted to the saints' (Jude 3). That can still be a hazardous exercise, as some have found. It can cost friendships, reputations, promotion, popularity and even one's job. But such is the courage required of true shepherds.

Tenderness

The element of toughness, inherent in the work of the ancient shepherd, must be held in tension with the need for tenderness. The one must be matched by the other. The shepherd who rejoices in being tough might well end up not protecting the sheep but harming them and impairing their healthy growth in Christ. Some sheep need the rod, but many more veer on the side of innocent silliness and require the staff to help them out of difficulties, set them on their feet and restore them to their proper place in the flock.

The gentleness of the image is beautifully captured by Isaiah

40:11, to which we have already referred. After the harsh years of the exile, God knew that the treatment Israel needed was not further punishment but tender love. The delicate affection God displayed to his people then, as he gathered them 'in his arms and [carried] them close to his heart', will often be the approach we are required to take too.

The full dimensions of this compassionate ministry are spelled out by Ezekiel, through whom God announces that he will relieve the counterfeit shepherds of their responsibilities and assume the role himself. He promises: 'I will search for the lost and bring back the strays. I will bind up the injured and strengthen the weak, but the sleek and the strong I will destroy. I will shepherd the flock with justice' (34:16). Searching for the lost speaks of the task of evangelism. Bringing back the strays speaks of the ministry of restoration. Binding up the injured focuses on the vocation of healing. Strengthening the weak stresses the task of nurturing, especially with good, luscious, green and nourishing food. The remainder of the verse reminds us that tenderness must not degenerate into sentimentality, and even tenderness must be dispensed, as is fitting in the service of a holy God, in a context of righteousness.

Pastoral ministry requires great discernment to know when toughness is appropriate and when tenderness is. Disaster follows if the two are confused and mistakenly applied.

Maintenance and mission

The image of the shepherd cuts through the false debates which often occur about whether the energies of the ministry should be directed primarily to those already in the church or to those outside. It teaches us emphatically that our responsibility is to both.

Different understandings of the church lead people to put the stress in different places. A traditional view of the church, as an established church in a nation, will lead to a pastoral model which emphasizes serving the baptized. A more sectarian approach, which has sometimes led historically to a preoccupation with serving the pious elect, more often leads to aggressive evangelism. From this perspective the church is often seen as a tiny vessel afloat on a stormy sea with the duty of rescuing as many as possible from the waves.[9] Recent days have seen a coming together of these perspectives as, in an increasingly post-Christian western world, the established church has gained a new understanding of its missionary situation and sectarian churches have grasped a greater need to care for those who are already members.

It should not have taken us so long to reach such balance, since it is inherent in the shepherd, the most foundational of all images of pastoral ministry.

Caring for those in the fold

Paul's charge to the Ephesian elders instructed them to 'keep watch over … all the flock of which the Holy Spirit has made you overseers' (Acts 20:28). His stress on the need to care for all is significant, at least in our contemporary context. Every self-respecting shepherd would be concerned that all his sheep were following him and were fed. Only an indolent, incompetent or unworthy shepherd would treat the flock with a careless indifference which allowed some of its members to go wandering off on their own. If that happened, the irresponsible shepherd would pay for it when he returned to the owner of the sheep. This is the very point Paul makes. The sheep have been purchased by the blood of Christ and, consequently, are owned by him (v. 28 and 1 Cor. 6:19–20). Caring for them, then, is a matter of looking after them not only for their own sakes but for the sake of the one to whom they belong. That puts an even higher premium on the responsibility of the shepherd.

If this is so, then it is not for us to pick and choose those for whom we will care. We have a privilege entrusted to us by God, and it is essential that we steward it meticulously. How different this is from the approach of some who willingly ditch difficult sheep, or show little concern for the slower sheep who either cannot or will not keep up. Flocks have been divided and many ejected from the fold, even if not explicitly, because they didn't fit in with the way the church was going. Some of the practices of aggressive task-orientated leadership have left the sheep feeling used but not cared for, while others have exercised a rigorous selection process before people have been allowed to join, or remain, in their flock. Of course, people leave particular folds and transfer to others. Some, sadly, as is evident from the later New Testament letters, leave the fold altogether. But they should leave as a result of their own choice rather than as a result of our failure to care. Like the shepherd, we need to count the sheep to ensure we have not lost any.

Caring for the sheep is a demanding and multi-faceted task. It involves not only finding pasture and feeding them, defending them from enemies and protecting them from dangers, but diagnosing their ills and curing them from their diseases, and, these days, engaging in preventative measures, like the sheep dip, that will save them from future ailments. Ezekiel gave us an insight into the variety of care needed. Restoring, teaching, encouraging, listening, healing, counselling, rebuking, strengthening and exhorting will all be called into play.

John 10:14 highlights another important aspect of the character of the good shepherd. He has a sound knowledge of his sheep. One cannot minister effectively to people one does not know. Ministering too abstractly is not generally characteristic of good shepherds. Sadly, many of us fail at this point. We are so caught up in church work and crisis ministry that we do not know sufficient about the particular individuals and the ordinary lives of those who are our members. Preachers are often criticized for not making the connection between the Bible and the real world in which people live, chiefly because we do not know them well enough. This is demonstrated, for example, in relation to the world of work. Many of our members spend most of their waking hours working, but we often totally ignore this when it comes to church, addressing, instead, an entirely different agenda made up of church issues. Yet, according to Ephesians 4:12, pastors are those who are supposed to be preparing 'God's people for works of service'. We should therefore be addressing the issues that concern them in their workplace and teaching much more about how to be Christians not in the church but in the world.[10]

Searching for those outside the fold

Demanding though it is to care for those already in the fold, the energies of the true shepherd cannot be wholly spent in doing so. A powerful aspect of the image of the shepherd is the search for lost sheep. The shepherd takes the initiative in going to find them because the sheep are incapable of taking that initiative for themselves. In doing so they epitomize the initiative God takes in finding lost sinners.

This aspect of the shepherd's role is clear in Scripture. When God seized the role of the shepherd away from the false shepherds, he emphasized that his was the gracious initiative in finding the lost sheep. 'I myself will search for my sheep ...' (Ezek. 34:11). 'I will rescue them from all the places where they were scattered ...' (v. 12). 'I will search for the lost and bring back the strays' (v. 16). The parable of the lost sheep (Luke 15:3–7) reverberates with the same melody of God's grace reaching out to those in need. A more problematic note, but on the same theme, is sounded in John 10:16 where Jesus says that he must gather in other sheep who are not of this sheep pen. In context this might well be a reference to Gentiles.[11] Whatever the exegesis of the phrase 'other sheep', the missiological thrust is abundantly clear. The point is that these sheep, whoever they are, must be brought in, and that requires the shepherd to go out and get them.

With this background, it is no surprise that Paul tells Timothy, while expounding the work of the pastor, that he was to 'do the work of an evangelist, discharge all the duties of your ministry' (2 Tim. 4:5). To do the work of a pastor necessarily involves doing the work of an evangelist. They are not in tension. Pastors who abdicate their work as evangelists cannot be faithful to their biblical calling. Moreover, they will be poorer as pastors, since they will neither be in touch with people on the outside of the church (where most of the church's members live and work), nor will they see the power of the gospel at work in the initial stages of conversion, nor are they likely to be able to communicate the truth of God's word in any meaningful way to the contemporary world. But our chief concern must be this: they will be failing to discharge their God-given duty and failing to imitate the model of the divine shepherd.

Shepherding is a dynamic image, not static. It's about mission as much as maintenance. Both are needed.

Already but not yet

A further dimension requires comment. The gospels draw attention to the role which the messianic shepherd will one day play in the final acts of history. The shepherd is both a contemporary and an eschatological figure.

The process of gathering in has begun

Shepherds are already at work, and rightly so. Sheep are currently being drawn into the fold and nurtured. The command to 'Tend my sheep' is properly being heeded, not by Peter alone, but by countless other pastors of the flock. There is no need to hold back. The commission has been issued (Matt. 28:19). So we can truthfully say that 'all over the world this gospel is bearing fruit and growing' (Col. 1:6). But that is only one side of the coin.

The process of separating is yet to come

Alongside all that is said about shepherding as a motif for Christian ministry throughout the age of the church, there is one aspect of the role that belongs uniquely to the great shepherd himself. The shepherd not only gathers but separates. The day will come when the Great Shepherd will play out the final act of history, which will be one of both salvation and judgment.

The image of the shepherd is alluded to as the gospels speak of that final act. There is a suggestion of it in Mark 13:27. The angels of the Son of Man 'will gather his elect from the four winds, from the ends of the earth to the ends of the heavens'. Those who have been scattered will ultimately be united in this closing climactic act of the Great Shepherd, whose role, according to the Old Testament prophets, is to gather, not scatter, the flock.

But the reference to the role of the shepherd in judgment is even more explicit in the parable of the sheep and the goats (Matt. 25:31–46). This conclusive act of the shepherd involves him in separating sheep from goats, earmarking the sheep to eternal life and assigning the goats to eternal punishment. He makes the separation between the two on the basis of what people have done 'for one of the least of these brothers and sisters of mine' (v. 40). In his court, it is not words that count but actions; actions which reveal what people really think about the disciples of Jesus and so, in turn, what they think of him. The good shepherd, then, has a function not only in caring for the sheep now but also in determining their eternal destiny then.

Costly but rewarding

The cost

The Bible seems to make no effort to avoid the small print in its job description of the shepherd. To be a shepherd is costly; to be a good shepherd may well cost one one's life. As the good shepherd, Jesus knew that he was required to lay down his life for his sheep (John 10:11). He did so in fulfilment of the prophecy of Zechariah that the sword would strike the shepherd and the sheep would be scattered (13:7). But he did so knowing that it was through laying down his life that the people of God would be fully restored in their relationship to him.

Some seek a ministry without cost. But it is a sheer illusion to imagine that anyone could ever pastor in the image of the good shepherd and avoid any cost. Cost is inherent in the role. The costs may differ from time to time and place to place. Most pay the cost of working long and unsociable hours, of being vulnerable, of being weak, of facing criticism, of being lonely, of being drained by people. Ministry takes it out of you. Others may be required to pay the greater cost of sacrificing their freedom or even their lives. Paying the cost is a sign of being an authentic shepherd. It's what Jesus did and what he calls us to do too.

The reward

And yet, if the cost is great, the reward is greater. No role can be as rewarding as that of the shepherd. The sheer privilege of caring for the sheep, of seeing them found, nurtured, nourished and maturing, is difficult to surpass. The intimacy of the relationship between shepherd and sheep, especially during those most vulnerable and most joyous occasions in life, cannot be bettered. The wonder of serving the great shepherd and working under his direction cannot be surpassed. The unworthy and needy under-shepherd serves knowing that 'the God of peace, who through the blood of the eternal covenant brought back from the dead our Lord Jesus, that great Shepherd of the sheep, [will] equip [us] with everything good for doing his will, and ... work in us what is pleasing to him, through Jesus Christ, to whom be glory for ever and ever. Amen' (Heb. 13:20–21). One day, that great and good shepherd will pass his verdict on our ministries and we shall receive 'the crown of glory that will never fade away' (1 Pet. 5:4). In the meantime we are called to be faithful, and to be fruitful, to pay the cost and keep our eye on the reward.

Questions for reflection

1. How far can I testify that 'The Lord is my shepherd'? What does it mean to me?

2. Does 1 Peter 5:2–4 characterize my ministry?

3. In what ways does my present ministry call for courage?

4. Am I serving 'all the flock of God' for which I am responsible, or only part of it?

5. Both mission and maintenance are vital. Do I major on one at the expense of the other? If so, how can I bring about a better balance in my ministry?

6. Do I do the work of an evangelist? When did I last witness to someone or lead someone to faith in Christ? Or am I content to leave that to someone else?

7. What is my attitude towards the cost of ministry? Do I accept it joyfully, deny it or resent it? What is the healthiest way to deal with it?

Notes

Introduction

[1] This book speaks mostly in terms of full-time church pastors or ministers. But it also has other kinds of church leader in mind. Most, perhaps all, of what it has to say is applicable just as much to the house-group leader, the deacon, the worship leader, the evangelist, the lay reader, the youth-group leader, and so on.

[2] Recent legal decisions have, in fact, ruled that in the UK vicars and ministers are office holders, not employees of the church. Employed only by God, the legal redress available to other employees through employment tribunals or the courts is not open to them.

[3] For an insightful and autobiographical approach to this contrast see David Hansen, *The Art of Pastoring: Ministry Without All the Answers* (Downers Grove: IVP, 1994). Hansen says, 'Here's what pastoral ministry is for me: Every day, as I go about my tasks as a pastor, I am a follower of Jesus. *I am therefore a parable of him to those I encounter.* The parable of Jesus works the power and presence of Jesus in their lives' (p. 28).

[4] Paul Beasley-Murray, *Power for God's Sake* (Carlisle: Paternoster, 1998), pp. 34–37 and 86.

[5] David W. Bennett has recently set out a full list of them, carefully arranged and tabulated, in *Metaphors of Ministry: Biblical Images for Leaders and Followers* (Carlisle: Paternoster, 1993).

[6] London: Darton Longman and Todd, 1984.

[7] Nashville: Abingdon, 1989.

[8] Grove Pastoral Series no. 54; Cambridge: Grove Books, 1993.

[9] *Ibid.*, pp. 23f.

[10] London: Hodder and Stoughton, 1993.

[11] Thomas C. Oden, *Care of Souls in the Classic Tradition* (Philadelphia: Fortress, 1984), p. 35.

[12] Bunting, *op. cit.*, pp. 5f.

[13] *Ibid.*, p. 5.

[14] Sallie McFague, *Metaphorical Theology* (Philadelphia: Fortress, 1982, and London: SCM, 1983), p. 14. See further the excellent discussion in Colin Gunton, *The Actuality of the Atonement: A Study in Metaphor, Rationality and the Christian Tradition* (Edinburgh: T. and T. Clark, 1988), ch. 2.

[15] McFague, *ibid.*, p. 15.

[16] *Ibid.*, p. 26.

[17] Eugene H. Peterson, *Working the Angles: The Shape of Pastoral Integrity* (Grand Rapids: Eerdmans, 1987), pp. 74–86. His summary is: 'Contemplative exegesis, then, involves these two matters: an openness to words that reveal and a submission to words that shape. Words are double dimensioned: they carry meaning from their source and they carry influence to their destination' (p. 86).

[18] This differs from reader-response approaches to Scripture in that it takes seriously what the author intended to say and does not make the reader the starting-point.

[19] Edinburgh: T. and T. Clark, 1907.

[20] *Ibid.*, pp. 25f.

1. Ambassador

[1] A recent study of the role is to be found in Antony Bash, *Ambassadors for Christ: An Explanation of Ambassadorial Language in the New Testament* (Leiden: Mohr, 1997).

[2] He also speaks of himself as *presbytes* in Philemon 9. This could be translated 'ambassador', but is probably more correctly translated 'old man' as in the NIV. On the connection between the two, see later. Bash also explores Galatians 2:1–10 as an example of an embassy.

[3] Bash, *op. cit.*

[4] An ambassador is *presbytes* and an elder is *presbyteros*.

[5] Bash says this is typical of the work of the ambassador (*op. cit.*, p. 48).

[6] Ralph P. Martin, *2 Corinthians*, Word Biblical Commentary (Waco: Word, 1986), p. 156.

[7] Sidney Greidanus, *The Modern Preacher and the Ancient Text* (Leicester: Apollos, 1988), p. 9.

[8] See Bash, *op. cit.*, pp. 62–67.

[9] Markus Barth, *Ephesians 4 – 6*, Anchor Bible (New York: Doubleday 1975), p. 782.

[10] Bash cites some evidence of ambassador's being ill-treated and refers to the fact that Pompey secured the death of one hundred at one time. But these were not matters of which they boasted (*op. cit.*, p. 106).

[11] *The Times*, 29 July 1997.

[12] Peter Collier and David Horowitz, *The Kennedys* (London: Book Club Associates, 1985), p. 91.

[13] James Denney, *The Second Epistle to the Corinthians*, Expositor's Bible (London: Hodder and Stoughton, 1894), p. 186.

[14] *Ibid.*, p. 187.

[15] G. Bornkamm, *presbeuō*, *Theological Dictionary of the New Testament* VI, ed. G. Kittel (Grand Rapids: Eerdmans, 1968), p. 682.

16 *Op. cit.,* pp. 12f.

17 Reconciliation is obviously central to Paul, although not perhaps the primary trajectory of his gospel as argued by Ralph P. Martin in *Reconciliation: A Study in Paul's Theology* (London: Marshall, Morgan and Scott, 1981). It is this which Bash suggests is the place where Paul distinguishes himself most from other contemporary ambassadors in that they would not usually be engaged in seeking reconciliation (*op. cit.,* pp. 100–104).

18 Donald E. Messer, *A Conspiracy of Goodness: Contemporary Images of Christian Mission* (Nashville: Abingdon Press, 1992), p. 30.

19 Donald English, *An Evangelical Theology of Ministry* (Nashville: Abingdon, 1996), pp. 64f.

20 I owe this quotation, which comes from Wesley's sermon on 'Salvation by Faith', to Messer, *op. cit.,* p. 100.

21 *Op. cit.,* p. 113.

22 Cited in W. E. Chadwick, *The Pastoral Teaching of St Paul: His Ministerial Ideals* (Edinburgh: T. and T. Clark, 1907), p. 160.

2. Athlete

1 Charles Swindoll, *Growing Deeper in the Christian Life* (London: Hodder and Stoughton, 1988), p. 205.

2 Victor C. Pfitzner, *Paul and the Agōn Motif* (Leiden: E. J. Brill, 1967), p. 74. Pfitzner draws his conclusions from Josephus, *The Antiquities of the Jews* XV.viii.1.

3 *Ibid.,* p. 21.

4 *Ibid.,* pp. 23–27.

5 *Ibid.,* pp. 28–35.

6 *Ibid.,* pp. 38–48.

7 J. N. D. Kelly, *The Pastoral Epistles* (London: A. and C. Black, 1963), p. 176.

8 John Chrysostom, *Homilies on Timothy,* in Nicene and Post-Nicene Fathers XIII (Grand Rapids: Eerdmans, 1979), p. 488; quoted by Thomas Oden, *First and Second Timothy and Titus,* Interpretation (Louisville: John Knox, 1989), p. 165.

9 Timothy Morgan, 'Reengineering the Seminary', *Christianity Today* (24 October 1994), p. 75.

10 Linford Christie speaking on the BBC1 television series *The Human Machine.*

11 Pfitzer points out the significance of Romans 9:16 in this regard and comments on the need for keeping effort and divine resource in balance. He remarks, 'The effort of an athlete and his intentness are necessary to reach this goal. But to its attainment belong also self-restriction and renunciation. An "ethic of activism" finds no basis here' (*op. cit.,* p. 134).

12 David W. Bennett, *Metaphors of Ministry: Biblical Images for Leaders and Followers* (Carlisle: Paternoster, 1993), p. 144.

13 For an excellent consideration of this area see Stanley Grenz and Roy Bell, *Betrayal of Trust: Sexual Misconduct in the Pastorate* (Downers Grove: IVP, 1995).

14 Carl Lewis and Jeffrey Marx, *Inside Track* (London: Pelham, 1990), p. 11.

15 *Ibid.,* p. 13.

16 John Chrysostom describes the desire for popularity as 'that most terrible rock of vainglory'. And he warns successful preachers against taking applause too seriously because great harm would be done both to the preacher and to the congregation if he did. He points out how easy it is to get carried away with the desire for praise, even when we have no skill in preaching. The danger is that we provide such food as will suit their taste and 'purchase' the

'tumult of acclamation' (*On the Priesthood*, Nicene and Post-Nicene Fathers IX, Grand Rapids: Eerdmans, 1978, 3.9 and 5. 6).

[17] I. Howard Marshall, *1 and 2 Thessalonians*, New Century Bible, (London: Marshall, Morgan & Scott, 1983), p. 87.

[18] Pfitzner, *op. cit.*, p. 153.

3. Builder

[1] Howard A. Snyder, *New Wineskins: Changing the Man-Made Structures of the Church* (London: Marshall, Morgan and Scott, 1975), p. 54.

[2] For the development of these themes see Walter Brueggemann, *1 Kings* and *2 Kings*, Knox Preaching Guides (Atlanta: John Knox, 1982).

[3] G. Kittel (ed.), *Theological Dictionary of the New Testament* V (Grand Rapids: Eerdmans, 1967), p. 137.

[4] David Peterson, *Engaging with God: A Biblical Theology of Worship* (Leicester: Apollos, 1992), p. 207. This chapter owes much to the summary Peterson gives of building terminology in a section on 'edification and the church'.

[5] *Ibid.*, pp. 207f.

[6] See further David W. Bennett, *Metaphors of Ministry: Biblical Images for Leaders and Followers* (Carlisle: Paternoster, 1993), p. 145.

[7] Edmund P. Clowney, *The Message of 1 Peter*, The Bible Speaks Today, (Leicester: IVP, 1988), p. 87.

[8] Exeter: Paternoster, 1978.

[9] I owe this point to D. A. Carson in *The Cross and Christian Ministry: An Exposition of Passages from 1 Corinthians* (Leicester: IVP, 1993), p. 78.

[10] Gordon D. Fee, *The First Epistle to the Corinthians*, New International Commentary on the New Testament (Grand Rapids: Eerdmans, 1987), p. 139.

[11] William Willimon, 'The Culture is Overrated', in *Christianity Today* (19 May 1997), p. 27.

[12] Rick Warren, *The Purpose Driven Church* (Grand Rapids: Zondervan, 1995), p. 209. Warren says that he never preaches or teaches without thinking: 'Father, I love you and you love me. I love these people and you love these people. Love these people through me. This is not an audience to be feared, but a family to be loved. There is no fear in love; perfect love casts out all fear' (p. 212).

[13] See H. W. Hollander, 'The Testing by Fire of the Builders' Works: 1 Cor 3:10–15', *New Testament Studies* 40 (1994), p. 96.

[14] Carson, *op. cit.*, p. 80. The quotation highlights the difficulty in drawing too rigid a distinction between the foundation and the materials. Foundations and the way of building upon them are integrally related in this case. See J. Stanley Glen, *Pastoral Problems in First Corinthians* (London: Epworth, 1965).

[15] Hollander, *op. cit.*, p. 100.

[16] Carson, *op. cit.*, p. 79.

4. Fool

[1] 'Scum' would also fall into this category.

2 William Shakespeare, *King Lear*, Act 1, Scene 4.

3 *Ibid.*

4 Guinness is actually speaking here of a figure he calls 'the third fool'. The first fool is the morally stupid person, and the second fool is the 'fool for Christ' which Guinness distinguishes from this third fool. But, interestingly, he cites the apostle Paul as an example of both the second and third types of fool.

5 Os Guinness, *The Gravedigger File* (London: Hodder and Stoughton, 1983), p. 234.

6 Judith Gunn, *Dostoyevsky: Dreamer and Prophet* (Oxford: Lion, 1990), p. 117.

7 Cited by Alastair V. Campbell, *Rediscovering Pastoral Care* (London: Darton Longman and Todd, 1981), pp. 50f., from F. Dostoyevsky, *The Idiot*, tr. David Magarshack (Harmondsworth: Penguin, 1955), p. 149. This chapter owes much to Campbell's insights and exposition of 'wise folly'.

8 As a recent example, see Morris West's *The Clowns of God* (London: Hodder and Stoughton, 1981). The theme is that of a pope, Gregory XVII, who believes he has received a private revelation about the second coming and the end of the world. The cardinals are unable to handle a pope who claims such experiences and believe him to be a madman, a mystic or a dangerous fanatic. But the readers are left to wonder who the real fools are.

9 *Daily Telegraph*, 22 June 1991.

10 Campbell, *op. cit.*, p. 47.

11 Gordon Fee, *The First Epistle to the Corinthians*, New International Commentary on the New Testament (Grand Rapids: Eerdmans, 1987), p. 68.

12 Morna D. Hooker, *Not Ashamed of the Gospel: New Testament Interpretations of the Death of Christ* (Carlisle: Paternoster, 1994), p. 8.

13 Quoted by Donald Coggan in *Cuthbert Bardsley: Bishop, Evangelist, Pastor* (London: Collins, 1989), p. 246. He also quotes Charles Kingsley as talking of 'true wisdom that shows itself by simplicity'.

14 Campbell, *op. cit.*, pp. 58f.

15 See Anthony Russell, *The Clerical Profession* (London: SPCK, 1980), for details.

16 Bryan Wilson, *Religion in a Secular Society* (London: Watts, 1966), pp. 125–141. Wilson first introduced the argument by saying that the clergy's activities were being seen by wider society as superfluous, and the clergy responded to this undervaluing of their role by inventing a specialism of their own, namely, ecumenism. But clerical response was more varied than this, and also included equipping themselves in social work or counselling in order to gain recognition by the wider society.

17 Thomas Oden, 'Recovering Pastoral Care's Lost Identity', in Leroy Aden and J. Harold Ellens (eds.), *The Church and Pastoral Care* (Grand Rapids: Baker, 1988), pp. 17–40. See also his *Care of Souls in the Classic Tradition* (Philadelphia: Fortress, 1984).

18 See ch. 7.

19 Campbell, *op. cit.*, pp. 54–58.

20 For a recent discussion of the question, see Ben Witherington III, *Conflict and Community in Corinth: A Socio-Rhetorical Commentary on 1 and 2 Corinthians* (Carlisle: Paternoster, 1995), pp. 343–350.

21 James Denney, *The Second Epistle to the Corinthians*, Expositor's Bible (London: Hodder and Stoughton, 1894), pp. 312f.

22 See Christopher Forbes, 'Comparison, Self-Praise and Irony: Paul's Boasting and the Conventions of Hellenistic Rhetoric', *New Testament Studies* XXXII (1986), pp. 1–30, and Ben Witherington III, *op. cit.*, pp. 432–441.

23 J. Paul Sampley, 'Paul, His Opponents in 2 Corinthians 10 – 13, and the Rhetorical

Handbooks', in *The Social World of Formative Christianity and Judaism*, ed. Jacob Neusner *et al.* (Philadelphia: Fortress, 1988), pp. 162–177.

[24] Forbes, *op. cit.*, pp. 8–10, and Victor Furnish, *II Corinthians*, Anchor Bible (New York: Doubleday), p. 554.

[25] John Calvin, *The Second Epistle of Paul the Apostle to the Corinthians, and the Epistles of Timothy, Titus and Philemon* (Edinburgh and London: Oliver and Boyd, 1964), p. 153.

[26] Furnish, *op. cit.*, p. 542.

[27] Ernest Best, *Second Corinthians,* Interpretation (Atlanta: John Knox, 1987), p. 114.

[28] Tring: Lion, 1982.

5. Parent

[1] A trite example of this is a sermon on Isaiah 6 which would be based on the three points 'Woe ... Lo ... Go.' It works only if you are using the AV! The more serious error of preachers is to connect a number of passages together which use the same English word, but which translate different Greek words and do not relate in the same way in the original.

[2] I owe this to Abraham J. Malherbe, '"Gentle as a Nurse": The Cynic Background to 1 Thess ii', *Novum Testamentum* 12 (1970), pp. 205–210. The first part of this chapter is based on his article and also on his *Paul and the Thessalonians* (Philadelphia: Fortress, 1987).

[3] 'Gentle as a Nurse', p. 211.

[4] Malherbe comments on the large number of tomb inscriptions which lovingly describe the kindness of nurses. But he acknowledges that the picture was not unequivocal.

[5] Malherbe, *Thessalonians, op. cit.,* p 59.

[6] 'Gentle as a Nurse', p. 213.

[7] Plutarch, *How to Tell a Flatterer from a Friend,* cited in Malherbe, *Thessalonians*, p. 55.

[8] Some may find Paul's way of speaking about the role of mother and father to be culture-bound and gender-stereotyping. But our aim is to understand what Paul wrote and then to ask about its relevance for the fully rounded pastoral role, not to endorse particular stereotypes of maternal or paternal behaviour.

[9] I. Howard Marshall, *I and II Thessalonians*, New Century Bible (London: Marshall, Morgan and Scott, 1983), p. 71.

[10] Philip Hacking, *The Spirit is Among us: Personal Renewal and the Local Church* (Basingstoke: Marshall Pickering, 1987), p. 20.

[11] John Calvin, *Epistles of Paul to Romans and to the Thessalonians*, Edinburgh: St Andrew Press, 1961, p. 344.

[12] Eva Lassen, 'The Roman Family: Ideal and Metaphor', in *Constructing Early Christian Families: Family as Social Reality and Metaphor*, ed. Halvor Moxnes (London and New York: Routledge, 1997), p. 107.

[13] See further Ernest Best, *Paul and his Converts* (Edinburgh: T. and T. Clark, 1988), pp. 29–58; Stephen Joubert, 'Managing the Household: Paul as *Paterfamilias* of the Christian Household Group in Corinth', in Philip Esler (ed.), *Modelling Early Christianity: Social-Scientific Studies of the New Testament in its Context* (London and New York: Routledge, 1995), pp. 213–223; and for an older survey as it relates to preaching, John Stott, *The Preacher's Portrait* (1961; Leicester: IVP, 1995), pp. 71–88.

[14] For these quotations and a fuller exposition see Derek Tidball, *Skilful Shepherds: Explorations in Pastoral Theology* (1986; Leicester: Apollos, 1997), pp. 157–161.

15 Best, *op. cit.*, p. 37.

16 Abraham Malherbe, 'Pastoral Care in the Thessalonian Church' *New Testament Studies* 36 (1990), pp. 386f.

17 A fuller exposition of the point is prohibited by space here, but it can be amply followed up, not least as it relates to pastoral ministry, in John R. W. Stott, *Your Mind Matters* (London: IVP, 1972), especially pp. 41–43, and the works he cites.

18 A full examination of this can be found in W. P. De Boer, *The Imitation of Paul* (Kampen: J. H. Kok, 1962). See also Best, *op. cit.*, pp. 59–72, and Tidball, *op. cit.*, pp. 108–109.

19 Cited by Best, *op. cit.*, p. 61.

20 James Denney, *The Epistles to the Thessalonians*, Expositor's Bible (London: Hodder and Stoughton, 1899), p. 77.

6. Pilot

1 *Daily Telegraph*, 17 July 1990.

2 Alexander Maclaren, *The Gospel According to John* (London: Hodder and Stoughton, 1907), 3, pp. 357–358. Quoted in Bruce Milne, *The Message of John*, The Bible Speaks Today (Leicester: IVP, 1993), p. 315.

3 Quoted by Thomas Oden in 'Historical Pastoral Care Tradition', *Journal of Psychology and Theology* 20 (1992) p. 142. No wonder Oden comments that here is the task of the soul guide 'under the metaphor of a no-nonsense navigator: tough, aware, and trim'.

4 In quoting this passage I am not endorsing it in its details, but merely using it to illustrate the way the early church sometimes thought. To suggest that the laity are passengers, as if they had no part to play in the running of the ship, is very deficient!

5 Clementina, *The Epistle of Clement to James*, Ante-Nicene Fathers VIII, pp. 220–221. Quoted in Thomas Oden, *Becoming a Minister*, Classical Pastoral Care (New York: Crossroad, 1987), p. 85.

6 L. W. J. Fifield, *Navigation for Watchkeepers* (London: Heinemann, 1980), p. 1. I owe this quotation and some other ideas in this chapter to my friend and student Graham Wilburn, who has had long experience in responsible positions at sea.

7 Lionel Casson, *Ships and Seamanship in the Ancient World* (Princeton: Princeton University Press, 1971), pp. 300–302, 307, 310, 316.

8 'Despite the duties and obligations of a pilot, his presence on board does not relieve the master or officer in charge of the watch from their duties and obligations for the safety of the ship' (Fifield, *op. cit.*, pp. 53 and 57).

9 Oden, *Becoming a Minister*, p. 85.

10 John Chrysostom, *On the Priesthood* III.vii, Nicene and Post-Nicene Fathers IX (Grand Rapids: Eerdmans, 1978. The same point is made by Gregory Nazianzen in his funeral oration for St Basil.

11 *Ibid.*

12 For introductions to postmodernism see Stanley Grenz, *A Primer on Postmodernism* (Grand Rapids: Eerdmans, 1996); David Lyon, *Postmodernity* (Milton Keynes: Open University Press, 1994); Richard Middleton and Brian Walsh, *Truth is Stranger than it Used to Be* (London: SPCK, 1995) and George Veith, *A Guide to Contemporary Culture* (Leicester: Crossway, 1996).

13 Dave Tomlinson, *The Post Evangelical* (London: Triangle, 1995). But see also Graham Cray *et al.*, *The Post-Evangelical Debate* (London: SPCK, 1997), and especially the chapters by

Graham Cray and Nigel Wright which raise serious questions about post-evangelicalism, and, in my view, rightly so.

[14] Quoted in Paul Beasley-Murray, *Dynamic Leadership* (Eastbourne: MARC, 1990), p. 24.

[15] Chrysostom, *op. cit.*

7. Scum

[1] *The Message* (Colorado Springs: NavPress, 1993), p. 405.

[2] Bruce J. Malina, *The New Testament World: Insights from Cultural Anthropology* (London: SCM, 1983), p. 32. Full details are to be found on pp. 25–50.

[3] C. K. Barrett, *The First Epistle to the Corinthians,* Black's New Testament Commentaries (London: A and C. Black, 1968), p. 112.

[4] For details see Stahin, *peripsēma,* in *Theological Dictionary of the New Testament* VI, ed. G. Kittel (Grand Rapids: Eerdmans, 1968), pp. 84–91, and Hauck, *perikatharma,* in *ibid.* III, pp. 430f. Gordon Fee rightly exercises some caution as to how far this idea should be pressed. See *The First Epistle to the Corinthians,* New International Commentary on the New Testament (Grand Rapids: Eerdmans, 1987), p. 180.

[5] Meic Pearse, *Who's Feeding Whom?* (Carlisle: Solway, 1996), pp. 2f.

[6] For a simple introduction to the theory of 'over-realized eschatology' as an interpretative key to 1 Corinthians, see Anthony Thiselton, 'Realised Eschatology at Corinth', *New Testament Studies* xxiv (1978), pp. 510–526.

[7] On the somewhat difficult terminology of this verse, N. T. Wright comments, 'Paul is not adding to the achievement of Calvary. The word "afflictions" is never, in fact, used of the cross. He is merely putting into practice the principle of which Calvary was, in one sense, the supreme outworking. He understands the vocation of the church as being to suffer; he does not arrogate the privilege to himself, as though he were independent of Christ, but rightly sees that it is his precisely because it is Christ's, and so is he. This is what he means when he writes of suffering "with Christ" (Rom. 8:17) or of sharing in the fellowship of Christ's suffering.' For the reasoning that leads to this conclusion see *Colossians and Philemon*, Tyndale New Testament Commentaries (Leicester: IVP, 1986), pp. 87–89. This quotation is taken from p. 89.

[8] D. A. Carson, *The Cross and Christian Ministry* (Leicester: IVP, 1993), p. 109.

[9] The phrase is Alister McGrath's in *The Enigma of the Cross* (London: Hodder and Stoughton, 2nd edn) p. 102.

[10] Quoted in *ibid.,* p. 12.

8. Shepherd

[1] Thomas Oden, *Pastoral Theology: Essentials of Ministry* (San Francisco: Harper and Row, 1983), p. 49.

[2] For a more detailed consideration of the pastor as shepherd, see my book, *Skilful Shepherds: Explorations in Pastoral Theology* (2nd edn, Apollos, 1997).

[3] E. Beyreuther, 'Shepherd', in *New International Dictionary of New Testament Theology* III, ed. Colin Brown (Exeter: Paternoster, 1978), p. 565.

[4] Joachim Jeremias, *Jerusalem in the Time of Jesus* (London: SCM, 1969), pp. 302–305.

[5] On the varied imagery here in which a lamb can simultaneously be a lion, a sheep and a

shepherd, see G. R. Beasley-Murray, *The Book of Revelation*, New Century Bible (London: Oliphants, 1974), pp. 124–126 and 149.

6 John Stott, *The Message of Acts*, The Bible Speaks Today (Leicester: IVP, 1990), p. 329.

7 Alastair V. Campbell, *Rediscovering Pastoral Care* (London: Darton Longman and Todd, 1981), p. 27.

8 See Thomas Oden, *After Modernity What? Agenda for Theology* (Grand Rapids: Zondervan, 1992), pp. 21–29, for a stunning confession and analysis of theology's addiction to novelty.

9 This was the favourite image of D. L. Moody.

10 My colleague Mark Greene has done a good deal of research and writing in this area. He has devised a tool to enable pastors to assess and change their preaching to take such issues into account. It is called *The Three-Eared Preacher* and is available from the Open Learning Department, London Bible College, Green Lane, Northwood, Middx., HA6 2UW, UK. See also his *Thank God it's Monday* (Scripture Union, 2nd edn 1998).

11 It has become fashionable in some circles to argue that the other sheep are the followers of other religions. But there is no basis for that interpretation either in John, which is much concerned with the attitude of the Jews to Christian believers, or elsewhere in the New Testament.

GIVEN FOR YOU
A Fresh Look at Communion

ELEANOR KREIDER

Jesus gave us communion to be a central part of our Christian lives. Yet we often struggle to understand it and to give it a meaningful place. It can easily become 'mere ritual'. In *Given for you* Eleanor Kreider shows that this need not be the case. Much can be learned from the riches (and mistakes) of Christian history, and much can be done in the ways we celebrate communion today. She calls for a renewed unity of Word and Eucharist in Christian worship that recaptures its 'meal' character and truly forms the church in the image of Christ.

This book provides fresh and engaging material for pastors, teachers, worship-planners and leaders. Its graceful vision of the Lord's Supper as the central communal act of Christian worship will help the church flourish in an individualistic and selfish age.

'*A must for church leaders and all Christians.*'
Rev Joel Edwards, General Director, Evangelical Alliance, UK

'*Kreider opens us up to a whole new (or old!) way of seeing communion.* Given for you *roots our understanding in Scripture, is keenly aware of historical development, and is a valuable guide to contemporary practice.*'
Robert Webber, Professor of Theology, Wheaton College, and Director, Institute for Worship Studies

256 pages   Large Paperback

Inter-Varsity Press